Eating & D[...]

"This charming[...]
for every visitor to Italy.
~ Chicago Tribune

"an elegant, small guide..."
~ Minneapolis Star Tribune

Eating & Drinking in Spanish

•

"You may never point at a menu or
at someone else's plate again."
~ Chicago Tribune

"It makes dining...easy and enjoyable."
~ Toronto Sun

"It's small, unobtrusive...and artfully designed
- the perfect holiday gift."
~ Milwaukee Journal Sentinel

"Providing a depth that general phrasebooks lack."
~ Midwest Book Review

"A dietary dictionary to help you decipher 'ropa
vieja' as shredded beef, not old clothes!"
~ Caribbean Travel & Life

THE WHAT KIND OF FOOD AM I? SERIES

EATING &
DRINKING
IN FRANCE

French Menu Reader and Restaurant Guide

Andy Herbach and Michael Dillon

CAPRA PRESS
SANTA BARBARA

Thanks to Noel Young and David Dahl at Capra Press, Marian Olson (the best editor ever) and Mme. Marie Fossier (our helpful and thorough French editor). Dan Schmidt and Mark Berry, our "research assistants," deserve special thanks for their hard work eating and drinking their way through France.

These wonderful people all helped us with restaurant recommendations: Evelyne Coulon, Polly and Giles Daeger, John Dillon, Marie Fossier, Frank Frost, Loralyn Lasoued, Judy Penly and Tim Russell and Robert Ragir.

Cover design and illustrations
by Michael Dillon.

LIBRARY OF CONGRESS
CATALOGING-IN-PUBLICATION DATA

Herbach, Andy.
    Eating and drinking in France : French menu reader & restaurant guide / Andrew Herbach & Michael Dillon.
        p. cm. -- (What kind of food am I? series)
    ISBN 0-88496-442-6 (paper : alk. paper)
    1. Food--Dictionaries--French. 2. Cookery, French--Dictionaries--French. 3. French language--Dictionaries--English. 4 Restaurants--France--Guidebooks. I. Dillon, Michael. II. Title. III. Series.

TX350 .H36 2000
641.5944'03--dc21   00-023718

CAPRA PRESS
SANTA BARBARA
Post Office Box 2068
Santa Barbara, CA 93120

THE WHAT KIND OF FOOD AM I? SERIES

Eating & Drinking in France

Introduction

Can you imagine a foreign traveler who speaks basic English understanding what prime rib is? Or a porterhouse? Veggie platter, anyone? Buffalo wings? Sloppy joes?

Even people who speak passable French can have trouble reading a menu. The grand-sounding *suprême de volaille* is simply a chicken breast. *Cervelles* are brains, but *cervelle de canut* is a delicious herbed cheese spread found in Lyon.

They almost put a McDonalds here. Seriously.

Understanding the customs and food of a country helps travelers understand the people who live in the country.

If you love to travel as we do, you know the importance of a good guide. The same is true of dining. A good guide can make all the difference between a memorable evening and a dizzyingly bad one. This guide will help you find your way around a menu written in French. It gives you the freedom to enter places you might never have before and order a dinner without shouting, pointing and hand waving. Instead of fumbling with a bulky,

Le Hot Dog!

conspicuous tourist guide (most of which usually includes a very incomplete listing of foods), this pocket-sized book contains an alphabetical listing of food and drink commonly found on menus in French-speaking countries.

The real question is where are her eye brows anyway?

Of course, traveling to a foreign country means something different to everyone. For every vacation there are different expectations, different needs, and every traveler has his or her own idea of what will make that vacation memorable. For us, the making of a memorable vacation begins and ends with food.

Oh sure, the Louvre is great but have you ever had one of those long skinny hot dogs they sell in the little stands around Paris? They're bubbling hot, buried under a layer of delicately golden-brown Swiss cheese. We can't remember if we saw the Mona Lisa at the Louvre but we know for sure that we had one of those delicious hot dogs (not a thing like American hot dogs, not that we have anything against them) right after we came out of a grueling afternoon looking at art.

We know the panic of opening a menu without recognizing one word on it and the disappointment of being served something other

Love those pyramids!

7

than what you thought you'd ordered. On our first trip to Europe, we were served a plate of cold brains; we thought we had ordered chicken. This guide was created for the traveler who wants to enjoy, appreciate and experience authentic cuisine *and* know what he or she is eating.

Tire Bouchon.

The next time you find yourself seated in a bistro with the scent of roasted garlic in the air and an incomprehensible menu in your hands, simply pull this guide from your pocket and get ready to enjoy the delicious cuisine of France.

How to Use This Guide

In France, Belgium, Luxembourg, Switzerland and the French West Indies, the menu is almost always posted outside of the restaurant or in a window. This makes choosing a restaurant easy and fun as you "window shop" for your next meal.

Remember that the dish that you ordered may not be exactly as described in this guide. Every chef is (and should be) innovative. What we have listed for you in this guide is the most common version of a dish.

If a menu has an English translation it does not mean that the translation is correct. One travel writer, Margo Classé (*Hello France! A Hotel Guide to Paris and 25 Other French Cities*, ISBN 0-9653944-0-9, Wilson Publishing), once ordered beans and was served beets instead.

Often, a restaurant will offer several *menus fixes* (fixed price menus). These are always a better value than eating *à la carte*. Restaurants frequently offer a plate of the day (*plat du jour*) and some restaurants offer a set-price gourmet menu (*menu dégustation*) of specialties of the chef. The price of a meal will occasionally include the house wine (*vin compris*).

Green salads (*salades vertes*) are served after the main course and before dessert. Rarely is a salad included in the cost of a meal. Times have changed and you may now order a salad as an appetizer.

The French really love their dogs. It is not uncommon (no matter what type of eating establishment you are dining in) to find several dogs under tables.

We love this about the French!

Tipping

A service charge is almost always added to your bill (*l'addition*) in France, Belgium and Luxembourg. Depending on the service, it is sometimes appropriate to leave an additional 5 to 10%. The menu will usually note that service is included (*service compris*). Sometimes this is abbreviated with the letters s.c. The letters s.n.c. stand for *service non compris* and this means that the service is not included in the price and you must leave a tip.

You will sometimes find *couvert* or cover charge on your menu (a small charge just for placing your butt at the table).

Mealtimes

In France, Belgium and Luxembourg, lunch is served from noon to around 2 p.m., and dinner from 7 p.m. to 10 p.m.

Water

Europeans joke that you can tell a U.S. tourist from his fanny pack, clothes and ubiquitous bottle of mineral water. Tap water is safe in France. Occasionally, you will find *non potable* signs in restrooms (especially in the rest stops of highways). This means that the water is not safe for drinking.

Waiters and waitresses often bring *eau minérale* (mineral water) to your table. You will be charged for it, so if you do not want mineral water ask for *eau du robinet* or *une carafe d'eau* (tap water).

Types of Eating Establishments

Auberge: An inn serving food and drink. These are most often found in the country.

Bar à café: Coffee shop serving light meals. Don't be mislead by the name as they rarely serve alcohol.

Bistro: Smaller and less fashionable than a restaurant serving traditional, simple French cooking. Some are very similar to taverns or pubs.

Brasserie: Originally, this term referred to a beer hall, but today serves food and drink.

Buffet: Eating establishment usually found in railroad stations.

Cabaret: Dinner and a show.

Café: You can sit at one for hours and watch life go by. Serves alcoholic beverages and snacks. Some serve complete meals.

Carnotzet: Small family restaurants found in French-speaking Switzerland.

Charcuteries: Delicatessens serving take-out food.

Créperies: Popular for lunch, serving *crêpes* (filled thin pancakes).

Express: Any eating establishment with this name is usually a snack bar.

Fromagerie: Serves up to 400 official types of cheese.

Hostellerie: Upscale country restaurant.

Lolo: Found in the French West Indies, these are roadside or harbor-side shacks serving grilled foods (usually specializing in seafood and ribs).

Pâtisseries: Pastry shops.

Pizzerias: You can figure this one out yourself.

Relais: Country inn or restaurant.

Restaurant: We think you can also figure this one out.

Restoroute: Restaurant found on the highway.

Rôtisserie: Restaurant that usually specializes in roasted and grilled meats.

Salon de thé: Open mid-morning to late evening, serving light fare, salads, cakes, ice cream and, of course, tea.

Tabac: Bar where you can also buy cigarettes, tickets for public transportation, lottery tickets and phone cards.

Traiteur: Deli.

Dining Specialties:

FRANCE

If you've bought this book, or are standing in a bookstore reading it, you most likely are well-aware of the joys of French food.

For the French, dining is nearly a ritual. In its full-blown form, it begins with an aperitif, which in France is never wine, but a cocktail, a beer, or if you're feeling flush, champagne. This is often accompanied by an *amuse-gueule,* a little snack of some sort. This is followed by an hors d'oeuvre, a snack of a more grand proportion that might be hot or cold, such as soup or a vegetable salad dressed with mayonnaise and hard boiled eggs. Then comes an entrée, which is a first course - pasta, for instance - and then the main

course which will most likely be meat. The main course is often followed by a salad, but it is a simple green salad, generally without
even onions, dressed with a light vinaigrette. After this, just when
you think you will explode and have secretly unbuckled your belt,
the *serveur* arrives with selections from the cheese platter that are
followed by dessert, and, finally, coffee. But if you do not want to
follow the French protocol, don't. Even if the waiter seems to disap-
prove, do what you like. The French eat their salads after dinner, but
you're not required to. In a highly recommended restaurant, we
ordered a green salad before our meal that wasn't even on the menu.
The waitress raised an eyebrow, served it with a smile as though she
found it amusing, but seemed genuinely pleased that we enjoyed it.

Simple café dining is one of the pleasures of a trip to France. You
can learn more sitting in a café for an hour than spending the day in
a museum. In Paris, people-watching is like no other place in the
world. But if that's not your cup of tea, you can have a great lunch
on the run. Street vendors generally sell terrific food; you'll find
excellent hot dogs, *crêpes* and roast-chicken sandwiches all over
Paris. At lunch time, Parisians eating long, thin *baguettes* filled with
chicken, mayonnaise and sliced eggs seem to fill the streets. The
fare varies a bit in other parts of France, but is no less inviting or
delicious.

In the South of France, the cuisine is heavily influenced by Italian food
(as you might expect so close to the Italian border), and is a lot lighter,
with olive oil and tomatoes replacing butter and cream.

In the North of France, the food is generally heavier, even seafood
dishes. The food in Alsace-Lorraine, on the German border, is definitely Germanic in character. The Spanish influence is felt as you
get closer to the Western border with Spain. And in the opinion of
many, Burgundy offers the traveler the best in classic French cuisine,

with game dishes predominating in the fall.

This guide includes many regional specialties like the blue cheese of Languedoc, the sausages of Lyon and Auvergne, the duck of Dordogne, the seafood (especially oysters) and *crêpes* of Brittany, *bouillabaisse* in Provence, the lamb of Normandy, the beef dishes of Burgundy, and the sauerkraut and pastries of Alsace.

Just a word on wine: Be adventurous. Your dining experience can be heightened by ordering the (often less-expensive) local wines. It seems to us that when we ask for them, service is better, the staff is friendlier and the food often tastes better. This may be because we have shown an interest in the region and thus a bit more care is taken in preparing our meal, or perhaps the food just tastes better with the local wine. However, in Paris, where wines from every corner of France are available, order your wine and don't worry about the region.

A traveler will have a hard time finding a bad meal in France.

BELGIUM

Belgium is divided into French-speaking and Flemish-speaking regions. Belgian cuisine is similar to French. Hearty soups, pâté, rich sauces, game and beer are found on almost all menus. Some specialties are:

> *asperges à la flamande,* white asparagus w/egg sauce
> *carbonnade à la boeuf,* beef marinated in beer & cooked in onions & herbs
> *carbonnade à la bruxelloise,* pork in tomato/tarragon sauce
> *fricadelles à la bière,* meatballs in beer
> *fricassée liégeois,* fried eggs, bacon & sausage
> *gaufre,* waffle
> *jambon cuit d'Ardennes,* smoked ham

oie à l'instar de visé, goose boiled & then fried
potage au cerfeuil, soup of chervil & other herbs
rognons de veau à la liégeoise, roast veal kidneys
salade de liège, bean & potato salad
salade wallonie, warm salad w/lettuce, bacon & potatoes
truite à l'ardennaise, trout cooked in wine sauce
waterzooi, chicken or fish poached in sauce w/vegetables

LUXEMBOURG

Although the native tongue of Luxembourg is Luxembourgeois (Letzebuergesch), a mixture of old French and low German, almost everyone speaks German and French. French is the official language of the government. Similar to Belgian food, Luxembourg dishes feature sausages and sauerkraut. Some specialties are:
cochon de lait en gelée, suckling pig in aspic
jud mat gardebóneh, smoked pork & bean dish
quenelles de foie de veau, calf's liver dumplings
treipen, black pudding & sausages w/potatoes
tripe à la luxembourgeoise, tripe specialty

SWITZERLAND

Swiss orderliness and French style are found in French-speaking Switzerland (the Western part of Switzerland). The cuisine here is French. Lyon, one of France's gastronomic capitals, is only 100 miles away. All menus are influenced by German and Italian cuisine. The specialties of French-speaking Switzerland include:
abats, organ meats
andouillettes, tripe sausages
émincé de veau, slices of veal sauteed in butter & served
    w/cream sauce
omble chevalier, salmon-like trout found in Lake Geneva

longeole, pork sausage stuffed w/cabbage, leeks & spinach

petit salé, salt pork

truite meunière, trout lightly floured & fried in butter
(usually in a parsley & butter sauce)

Of course, the Swiss are famous for their chocolate.

FRENCH WEST INDIES

Guadeloupe, Martinique, the French side of St. Martin (the other side is Dutch), St. Barthélemy ("St. Barts") and the small islands of Marie-Galante, Désirade and Les Saintes make up the French West Indies (a little bit of France in the Caribbean). Martinique and Guadeloupe are *départements* of France and the citizens of the French West Indies enjoy the same benefits as all French citizens. The French West Indies are known for their French cuisine. French cuisine with a Creole influence makes for some of the most innovative dishes in the world. Some specialties are:

anguille, eel

blaff, spicy stewed fresh fish dish

calalou, "pepperpot" stew w/many ingredients

harengs fumés à la Créole, spicy smoked herring dish
flamed in rum

lambi, conch

matoutou de crabes, spicy sautéed crab meat dish

matelote, freshwater fish stew (usually eel) w/wine

ouassous, large crayfish

pâté en pot, mutton soup

planteurs, rum & fruit punches

potage à la crème de coco,
cream of coconut soup

ti punch, rum, lime & sugarcane syrup

'Ti punch.

The Ten Simple Rules of Dining In France

1. Avoid eating in a restaurant that has a menu written in English.

2. Don't be afraid. They can't and won't hurt you. They are not laughing at you, they aren't even thinking about you.

3. Don't ever call the waiter "garçon."

4. Try to make reservations.

5. Return to a restaurant. You will always be treated better because few travelers return to the same restaurant.

6. The French dine leisurely. Don't expect to have the same speed of service as at home.

7. Don't talk loudly. You will notice that the French speak softly. Running shoes, backpacks, "fanny" packs, and large, conspicuous guide books, cameras, and loud voices are like wearing a neon sign announcing that you are a tourist.

8. Stand your ground without being aggressive.

9. Stay away from *cervelles*!

10. Always be courteous. Remember that you are a guest in their country.

Bon Appétit

French Pronunciation Guide

If you are looking for a comprehensive guide to speaking French, this is not the right place. What follows are simply a few tips for speaking French and a very brief pronunciation guide.

It is always good to learn a few polite terms so that you can excuse yourself when you've stepped on the foot of an elderly lady or spilled your drink down the back of the gentleman in front of you. It's also just common courtesy to greet the people you meet in your hotel, in shops and restaurants in their own language.

Words can be linked by an apostrophe such as *ce est* (it is) which becomes *c'est*.

If a word ends in a consonant and that word is followed by a word that starts in a vowel, the consonant is linked to the vowel. So, *vous avez* (you have) is pronounced voozavay.

Remember, the final consonant in a word is silent (unless followed by an e).

a like in far

e like in open

é and ez like the a in rate

è like the e in bet

ê like eh as in *crêpe*

i like the i in machine

o like the o in not

ô like the o in wrote

u round your lips as to say oh, but say ee

an, am, en, em, ant, ent like the a in wand

au, eau like the o in okay

er at the end of a word sounds like the ay in day

in, im, ain, aim like the a in sank

ou like the oo in cool

oi like the wa in water

que like the cu in curve

qui like kee

un is pronounced uhn

c like a k before a, o, u and
consonants
c like an s before e and i
ch like sh
ç like the s in simple
g before a, o and u like in
good.
g like the s in pleasure before i
and e
gn like the ny in canyon
h is always silent
j like the s in measure
r like an r being swallowed
s like the s in step but when
between vowels, it is
pronounced like a z
ss like an s
zh like the s in measure

English to French

*This is a brief listing of some
familiar English foods and
food-related words that you
may need in a restaurant setting. It is followed by a list of
phrases that may come in
handy.*

allergic, allergique
anchovies, anchois
appetizer, hors d'oeuvre
apple, pomme

artichoke, artichaut
ashtray, cendrier
asparagus, aspèrge
bacon, lard
baked, cuit au four
banana, banane
beans, fève
beef, boeuf
beefsteak, bifteck/steak
beer, bière
beverages, boissons
bill, l'addition

In a bar after drinks, you ask
for *le count; l'addition* is for
larger, more complicated
transactions.

bitter, amer
boiled, bouilli
bottle (half), demi-bouteille
bottle, bouteille
bowl, bol
braised, braisé
bread, pain
bread roll, petit pain
breakfast, petit déjeuner
broth, consommé
butter, beurre

In general, bread is buttered
for breakfast but not for dinner. We have no idea why.

cabbage, chou

cake, gâteau
candle, chandelle
carrot, carotte
cereal, céréale(s)
chair, chaise
check, chèque
cheers, santé
cheese, fromage
cherry, cerise
chicken, poulet
chicken breast, suprême de volaille

> The white meat of chicken is often referred to as *aile*, the wing (and breast), while dark meat is *cuisse*, leg (and thigh).

chops, côtelettes, côtes
clams, palourdes
cocktail, cocktail
cod, morue
coffee, café
coffee (American-style), café américain
coffee w/milk, café crème (*café au lait* if you want a lot of milk)
coffee (black), café noir
coffee (decaf), déca/décafféiné
cold, froid
corn, maïs
cover charge, couvert
cucumber, concombre

cup, tasse
custard, crème anglaise
dessert, dessert
dinner, dîner
dish (plate), assiette
drink, boisson
duck, canard
eggs, oeufs
espresso, café italien/café express/un express
fish, poisson
fish soup, bouillabaisse (the famous seafood stew)
fork, fourchette
french fries, pommes frites (or just frites)
fresh, fraîche
fried, frit
fruit, fruits
game, gibier
garlic, ail
gin, gin
glass, verre
goat, chèvre
goose, oie
grapefruit, pamplemousse
grapes, raisins
green beans, haricots verts
grilled, grillé
ham (cooked), jambon (cuit)
ham (cured), jambon (de Parme)

hamburger, hamburger

honey, miel

hot, chaud

ice, glaçon

ice cream, glace

ice (on the rocks), avec des glaçons

ice water, l'eau glacée

included, compris

ketchup, ketchup

knife, couteau

kosher, casher/kascher

lamb, agneau

large, grand

lemon, citron

lettuce, laitue

little, petit/peu de...

> The French respond very well to hand gestures. Feel free to express little or big or nearly anything with your hands and fingers. They do it all the time.

liver, foie

lobster, homard

loin, longe (pork)
   aloyau (beef)

lunch, déjeuner

match, allumette

mayonnaise, mayonnaise

meat, viande

medium (cooked), à point

melon, melon

menu, carte

milk, lait.
   Lait écrémé is skim milk
   & *lait entier*, whole milk

mineral water, eau minérale

mineral water (sparkling), eau minérale (gazeuse)

mineral water (w/out carbonation), eau minérale plate (non gazeuse)

mixed, mélange, mixte, mesclun (salad greens)

mushrooms, champignons

mussels, moules

mustard, moutarde

napkin, serviette

noodles, nouilles/pâtes

nuts, noix

octopus, poulpes

oil, huile

olive oil, huile d'olive

olives, olives

omelette, omelette

on the rocks (w/ ice), avec des glaçons

onions, oignons

orange, orange

orange juice, jus d'orange

overdone, trop cuit

oysters, huîtres

partridge, perdrix

pastry, pâtisserie

peaches, pêches
pears, poires
peas, petits pois
pepper (black), poivre
peppers (sweet), poivrons
perch, perche
pineapple, ananas
plate (dish), assiette
please, s'il vous plaît
plums, prunes
poached, poché
pork, porc
potatoes, pommes de terre
poultry, volaille
prawns, grosses crevettes
quail, caille
rabbit, lapin
rare, saignant

Saignant will be really hideously bloody; *à point*, what the French think of as medium, is more like we think of as rare.

raspberry, framboises
receipt, note
rice, riz
roast, rôti
rolls, petits pains
salad, salade
salmon, saumon
salt, sel
sandwich, sandwich(e)
sauce, sauce

sautéed, sauté
scallops, coquilles
(Saint-Jacques)
scrambled, brouillé
seafood, fruits de mer
seasonings, condiments
/assaisonnement
shellfish, crustacés
shrimp, crevettes
small, petit
smoked, fumé
snails, escargots
sole, sole
soup, soupe
spaghetti, spaghetti
sparkling (wine), champagne
specialty, spécialité
spicy, épicé
spinach, épinards
spoon, cuiller/cuillère
squid, calmar/calamar
steak, steak/bifteck
steamed, vapeur
stew, ragoût
strawberries, fraises
sugar, sucre
sugar substitute, édulco-
rant/de l'aspartam
supper, souper
sweet, doux/sucré
table, table
tea, thé

tea w/lemon, thé citron
tea w/milk, thé au lait
thank you, merci
tip, pourboire

Tipping is not common in
France. Waiters are well-paid,
and most tips are included; we
still always leave something.

toast, pain grillé
tomato, tomate
toothpick, cure-dents
trout, truite
tuna, thon
turkey, dindon/dinde
utensil, couvert
veal, veau
vegetable, légume
vegetarian, végétarien
venison, venaison
vinegar, vinaigre
vodka, vodka
waiter, monsieur
    (never *garçon*)
waitress, madame
    or mademoiselle
water, eau
watermelon, pastèque
well done, bien cuit. Very well
    done is *très bien cuit*
whipped cream, crème chan-
    tilly *(shan-tee-ee)*
wine, vin

wine list, carte des vins
wine (red), vin rouge
wine (rosé), vin rosé
wine (white), vin blanc
with, avec
without, sans
yogurt, yaourt

---

please, s'il vous plaît
thank you, merci
yes, oui
no, non

Bonjour is used as hello all the
time, even in the evening.
Bonsoir is used if you are
leaving, *bonne nuit* if you are
actually going to bed.

good morning, bonjour
good afternoon, bonjour
good evening, bonsoir
good night, bonne nuit
goodbye, au revoir
Do you speak English?,
    parlez-vous anglais?
I don't speak French, je ne
    parle pas français
excuse me, pardon
I don't understand, je ne
    comprends pas

It is a good idea to follow any
request or phrase, with *m'sieur,
madame* or *madamoiselle.*

I'd like a table, je voudrais une table

I'd like to reserve a table, je voudrais réserver une table

for one person, pour une personne

for two, pour deux
trois (3), quatre (4), cinq (5), six (6), sept (7), huit (8), neuf (9), dix (10)

this evening, ce soir

tomorrow, demain

near the window, près de la fenêtre

It's going to be smoky, so don't be afraid to ask to sit near the window and be sure to follow it with *s'il vous plait.*

with a view, avec vue

outside on the patio, sur la terrace

no smoking, non-fumeur
(don't count on this in France)

where is?, où est

where are?, où sont

the bathrooms, les toilettes

the bill, l'addition

a mistake (error), une erreur

Is service included?, Le service est-il compris?

It almost certainly will be.

Do you accept credit cards?, acceptez-vous les cartes de crédit?

traveler's checks, chèques de voyage (don't use these)

How much is it?, c'est combien?

What is this?, qu'est-ce que c'est?

I did not order this, ce n'est pas ce que j'ai commandé

This is, c'est

too, trop

cold, froid

hot, chaud

not fresh, n'est pas frais

rare, saignant

undercooked, pas assez cuit

overcooked, trop cuit

delicious, délicieux

I am a vegeterian, Je suis végétarien(ne)

without meat, pas de viande/sans viande

closed, fermé

Monday, lundi

Tuesday, mardi

Wednesday, mercredi

Thursday, jeudi

Friday, vendredi

Saturday, samedi

Sunday, dimanche

abats, abattis, organ meats
abricot, apricot
acras/accras, *beignets,* usually stuffed w/seafood, found in the French West Indies
acidulé, acidic
addition (l'addition), check/bill
affinée, aged
agneau, lamb
agneau de lait, milk-fed lamb
agneau pré-salé, lamb grazed on salt marshes
agrumes, citrus fruits
aiglefin, haddock

agneau.

aïgo bouido, garlic soup (means "boiled water")
aigre, sour
aigre-doux, sweet & sour
aigrelette, a sour sauce
aiguebelle, herbal after-dinner drink similar to *Chartreuse*
aiguillette, thin slice. *Aiguillette de boeuf* are slices of steak
ail, garlic
aile, wing of poultry
aile de raie, ray fin (a kite-shaped fish also called skate)
aile et cuisse, *aile*: literally wing, it means white meat in fowl; *cuisse*: literally leg, it means dark meat in fowl
aillade, garlic mayonnaise (see *aïoli*)
aillade gasconne, veal w/garlic found in southwest France
aïoli/ailloli, garlic mayonnaise. Found in many provençal dishes
aïoli garni, *aïoli* served w/boiled food, salt cod, vegetables & eggs
airelle, cranberry
airerons, wings
à la, à l', au, aux, in the manner of, in, with
à la carte, side dishes (each item ordered separately)
albert, a sauce of egg yolk, cream, horseradish, shallots & mustard
albuféra, *béchamel* sauce w/sweet peppers

alcool, alcohol

algues, seaweed

ali baba, spongecake soaked in rum

aligot, garlic mashed potatoes w/cheese

alimentation, food/food store

allumettes, puff pastry or potato strips

alose, shad (fish)

alouette, lark

alouette sans tête, rolled veal slice
    stuffed w/garlic & minced meat

aloyau, sirloin

Alsace, located in the Northeast corner of France (along the
    German border) is one of France's wine regions specializ-
    ing in dry white wine such as Gewürztraminer, Riesling,
    Pinot Gris, Pinot Blanc, Pinot Noir & Sylvaner

alsacienne, usually garnished w/sausage & sauerkraut (means
    "Alsace style")

amande, almond

amande de mer, small shellfish

amandine, w/almonds

amer/amère, bitter

américaine, white wine sauce usually w/brandy,
    shallots, tomatoes & garlic w/shrimp/lobster

Amer Picon, aperitif (wine & brandy w/herbs)

amidon, starch. *Amidon de blé* is cornstarch

amourettes, the bone marrow of an ox or calf

amuse-bouche, appetizer

amuse-gueule, appetizer

ananas, pineapple

anchoïade, anchovy spread from Provence

anchois, anchovy

ancienne, "old style": usually means a wine cream sauce
    w/mushrooms, shallots or onions

andalouse, usually w/eggplant, tomatoes & green peppers

andouille, tripe sausage

andouillette, small tripe sausage

[handwritten note:] Alouette was reported to be the last meal of Francois Mitterand, none the less it is illegal to sell in France.

[handwritten note:] Anana. The symbol of Welcome.

25

aneth, dill

angélique, the crystallized stalks of the herb angelica
  (a decoration for cakes)

anglaise, boiled/boiled or steamed vegetables/breaded, fried
  meat, fish or vegetables

anguille, eel. Many dishes in the French West Indies feature eels

anguille au vert, eel in a white sauce w/parsley

anis, aniseed

apéritif, drink before dinner

à point, medium rare

appellation d`origine contrôlée, an officially recognized wine
  of France. Sometimes designated by A.O.C. The makers of
  A.O.C. are the best of the French wine industry

arachide, peanut

araignée de mer, spider crab

ardennaise, usually means served w/berries ("Ardennes style")

ardoise, specials are often written on the *ardoise*, a chalk board.
  This can also mean (for regular customers) that they put it
  on your running bill

arête, fish bone

argenteuil, asparagus soup

arlequin, two flavors

armagnac, brandy (similar to *cognac*). The main difference is
  cognac is distilled twice (& thus smoother)
  while *armagnac* is distilled only once

armoricaine, in a tomato sauce

arôme, aroma

aromates, herbs & spices

aromatisé, flavored

artichaut, artichoke

artichauts à la barigoule, artichokes w/mushrooms & pork

artichaut violet, small artichoke

asperge, asparagus

asperge à la flamande, white asparagus w/egg sauce.
  A Belgian specialty

asperge d'Argenteuil, large white artichoke

aspic, gelatin
aspic de volaille, chicken in aspic
assaisonnement, dressing/seasoning
assiette, plate
assiette anglaise, cold cuts
assiette de charcuterie, assorted meat products (cold cuts)
assiette de crudités, a plate of raw vegetables
assiette du pêcheur, assorted fish plate
assorti, assorted
asturienne, w/livers
au, in
aubergine, eggplant
aulx, garlic (the plural of *ail*)
aumônière, *crêpe* filled & wrapped into the shape of a little
      purse. The word means "beggar's purse"
aurore, a tomato sauce
auvergnat, usually means served w/sausage & cabbage (means
      "Auvergne style")
aux, with
avec, with
avec des glaçons, on the rocks
avocat, avocado
avoine, oats
aziminu, Corsican *bouillabaisse*
baba au rhum, spongecake soaked in rum
bäckaoffa, meat & potato stew from Alsace
bacon, Canadian bacon
baeckeoffe, baked meat &
      potato stew from Alsace
bagna cauda, hot anchovy dip from Provence
baguette, long & thin loaf of bread
baies, berries
baigné, bathed
ballottine (de volaille), boned meat (poultry) stuffed, rolled,
      cooked &served in gelatine
banane, banana

au jus means with juice (handwritten annotation)

Same word for lawyer. Hmm. Avocat. (handwritten annotation)

Bäckaoffa... sounds kind of hostile. (handwritten annotation)

27

bananes flambées, bananas flamed in brandy

bananes vertes, green bananas used in dishes in the French West Indies

Bandol, popular wine from Provence. The red is full-bodied & spicy & the white is fruity, often with a hint of aniseed

banon, cheese from Provence dipped in *eau-de-vie* & wrapped in chestnut leaves

bar, bass

barbarie, Barbary (a type of duck)

barbouiado, vegetable *ragoût*

barbue, brill (fish)

barde, the lard or bacon put over roasts

barigoule, artichoke hearts, sausage, bacon, garlic & mushroom dish

baron, the hindquarter & leg of a lamb

barquette, small boat-shaped pastry. *Une barquette* means "a carton of"

Barry, à la du, served w/a cauliflower & cheese sauce

basilic, basil

basquaise, served w/tomatoes, or red peppers ("Basque style")

bâtard, a small *baguette*

batonnets, crisp sticks. *Batonnets de courgette* are crisp zucchini sticks

baudroie, monkfish. This can also refer to a fish soup w/garlic & vegetables

bavaroise, custard dessert

bavette, flank steak

béarnaise, *hollandaise* sauce w/vinegar, tarragon, shallots & wine

monkfish is a shark

béatilles, mixed organ meats

beaufort, a hard cheese

Beaujolais, one of France's wine regions (on the south tip of Burgundy) noted for fruity red wines. *Beaujolais Nouveau* is light & fruity & denotes the first wine to be released

beaumont, a mild cheese

bécasse, woodcock

bécassine, snipe

béchamel, white sauce (usually butter, milk
    (&/or cream) & flour)

beckenoff, pork & mutton baked w/potatoes

beignet, fritter filled w/fruit, meat &/or vegetables
    (a filled doughnut)

belle étoile, a mild cheese

belon, a type of oyster

bénédictine, dark green, brandy-based liqueur

bergamotte, a variety of lemon or pear

bercy, fish stock *velouté* w/white wine,
    shallots & parsley

berlingots, mint-flavored caramels

betterave, beet

beuchelle, creamed kidneys &
    sweetbreads

beurgoule, caramel-rice pudding

beurre, butter

beurre blanc, white butter sauce of
    white wine, vinegar & shallots

beurre blanc nantais, white butter & shallot sauce for fish

beurre d'ail, garlic butter

beurre d'anchois, anchovy butter

beurre de montpellier, green butter (made green from herbs)

beurre d'estragon, tarragon butter

beurre fondu, melted butter

beurre maître d'hôtel, butter w/chopped parsley & lemon juice

beurre manié, butter & flour thickening for sauces

beurre nantais, white butter

beurre noir, browned butter sauce (until it's almost black)

beurre noisette, lightly browned butter

bicard de soude, baking soda

biche, female deer

bien cuit, well done

bière, beer

bière à la pression, draft beer
bière blonde, lager beer
bière brune, dark beer
bière légère, light beer
bifteck, beef steak
biftek de cheval, horsemeat steak
bigarade, brown sauce usually w/vinegar, sugar & oranges
bigarreau, a type of cherry
bigorneaux, small sea mollusks
bigourneau, the shellfish periwinkle
billes de melons, melon balls
billy bi, cream of mushroom soup
biscotte, zwieback (sweetened bread enriched w/eggs baked & sliced & toasted until dry & crisp)
biscuit, biscuit/cookie
biscuit à la cuillère, ladyfingers
biscuit de Savoie, spongecake
biscuits aux brisures de chocolat, chocolate-chip cookies
bisque, chowder
bisque d'écrevisses, freshwater crayfish chowder
bisque de homard, lobster bisque
bisque de langoustines, saltwater crayfish chowder
blaff, spicy stewed fresh fish dish served in the French West Indies
blanc, white
blanc-cassis, white wine & black currant liqueur
blanc de blancs, white wine made from white grapes
blanc de poireau, the white part of a leek
blanc de volaille, boned breast of poultry
blanchaille, whitebait, a fish
blanchi, blanched
blanquette, stew (usually veal stew in a white sauce)

You may order a beer by simply asking for a "Pression" and indicate large or small with your hands.

Press-See-AHN

You'll find blaff all over the French West Indies. Love that name!

Blanc de volaille is rarely seen in France.

blanquette de veau, veal stew in a white sauce
blé, wheat
blé de turquie, corn
blé dur, duram wheat
blette, Swiss chard
bleu, blue cheese/meat prepared nearly raw/fish boiled very
    fresh. Some popular blue cheeses are bleu d'Auvergne,
    bleu de Bresse, bleu des Causses & bleu du Haut-Jura
blini, small pancakes (usually w/sour cream, caviar & salmon)
blonde, light (as in light-colored [lager] beer)
boeuf, beef
boeuf à la ficelle, beef cooked in stock
boeuf à la gardiane, beef & wine stew w/black olives
boeuf à la gordienne, braised beef dish from Provence
boeuf à la mode, beef marinated in red wine
boeuf bourguignon, beef stewed in red wine (burgundy)
    w/onions, bacon & mushrooms
boeuf braisé à la beauceronne, beef casserole found
    around Orléans
boeuf en daube, larded chunks of beef marinated & cooked in
    wine/beef casserole
boeuf miroton, beef stew or boiled beef w/onion sauce
boeuf mode, beef stew w/carrots. This can also refer to cold
    beef in jelly
boeuf salé, corned beef
bohémienne, eggplant & tomato
    casserole. A specialty in Nice
boisson, beverage
boissons compris, drinks included
boissons non compris, drinks not included
boîte, can, box or jar. *Une boîte de conserve...* means a can of...
boles de picolat, meatballs & mushrooms cooked in a sauce
bolet, boletus mushroom
bombe/bombe glacée, layered ice cream
bon, good
bonbons, candy

[handwritten note:] Boletus mushrooms are cêpes.

[handwritten note:] Bon Marché means a good deal

31

bonne femme, homestyle cooking. This can also refer to a *sauce velouté* w/*crème fraîche* & lemon juice

Bonne femme means good woman.

bonnefoy, *sauce velouté* w/shallots & white wine

Bordeaux, one of France's wine regions (the largest wine-producing area in the world). Red *Bordeaux* is made from a blend of cabernet sauvignon, merlot, cabernet franc, malbec & petite verdot grapes. White *Bordeaux* is made from semillon & sauvignon blanc grapes.

bordelaise, red wine sauce w/mushrooms, beef marrow & shallots

botte, bunch (as in a bunch of herbs). *Botte de radis* means bunch of radishes

bouchée, bite size

bouchée à la reine, puff pastry filled w/meat, seafood, sweet breads &/or mushrooms

boucherie, butcher shop. *Boucheries chevalines* are still found in France & are horsemeat butcher shops

bouchon, cork

boudin, blood sausage (black pudding)

boudin blanc, white sausage (sausage of white meats)

boudin liège, Belgian sausage

boudin noir (boudin antillais), spicy blood sausage (a specialty in the French West Indies)

Love boudin noir... of course we ate it without knowing what it was the first time.

bougon, a goat's milk cheese

bouillabaisse, shellfish & fish stewed in white wine, olive oil, saffron, tomatoes & garlic. There are many versions of this dish

bouilli, boiled/boiled beef

bouillon, broth/stock

boulanger, baker. *Boulangère* is a woman baker

boulangerie, bakery

boule de fromage frit, fried cheese ball

boulette, meatball or fishball

boulette de semoule, semolina & potato *gnocchi*

boulghour, bulgur wheat

boullinade, thick soup found in the South of France

bouquet, large (red) shrimp (usually served cold)

bouquet garni, a small bundle of herbs &/or spices tied
together in cheesecloth & used to provide flavor to dishes
while they cook

bouquet rose, prawns

bourbon, bourbon

bourboulhade, salt cod & garlic soup. Sometimes referred to as
a poor man's *bouillabaisse*

bourdaines, apples baked in pastry

bourdaloue, butter cake w/fruit

Bourgogne, Burgundy. Burgundy is one of France's wine
regions (famous for its red wines made from pinot noir
grapes)

Bourgueil, light, fruity wine from the Loire Valley

bourguignon/bourguignonne, mushrooms & onions in a red
wine sauce (see *boeuf bourguignon*)

bouribut, red wine duck stew

bourride, a fish stew found in the South of France (thickened
w/egg yolks & *aïoli*)

boursin, a mild, soft cheese

boutargue, smoked fish roe

bouteille, bottle

braisé, braised

braiser, to braise

branches de céleri, celery stalks

brandade, cod & potatoes dish

brandade de morue, salt cod w/garlic,
cream & olive oil

brandy, brandy

brebis, sheep's-milk cheese

brème, bream

Bretagne, Brittany

Bouteille

BOO-TAY

Bouteilles.

33

bretonne, usually a dish served w/white wine sauce or white beans ("Brittany style")

brézzolles, slices of veal

bricks, round, paper-thin sheets of pastry (usually filled w/egg & Middle Eastern spices). A specialty of Tunisia

brie, white, mellow, soft cheese. If you don't know what *brie* is, you shouldn't be in France

brins, branches or sprigs

brioche, small sweet cake or roll

broccio, a cheese (similar to *ricotta*) found in Corsica

broche, (on a) spit

brochet, pike

brochette de coeurs, heart kabab. A specialty in Toulouse

brochette, en, cooked on a skewer

brocoli, broccoli

broufado, braised beef w/anchovies

brouillade d'aubergines, stuffed eggplant w/tomatoes

brouillé, scrambled

Brouilly, red wine from Beaujolais

brousse de brebis, soft & mild sheep's- or goat's-milk cheese

brousse du Rove, cheese (similar to *ricotta*) made w/sheep's milk. The sheep graze on thyme which gives the cheese its unusual flavor

brugnon, nectarine

brûlé, burned/caramelized

brune, dark (as in dark beer)

brunoise, diced vegetables

brut, very dry

bûche de Noël, rolled Christmas cake

buffet froid, a variety of cold dishes

bugnes, fried doughnuts

buisson, vegetable dish

bulot, large sea snail

Burgundy, a wine (red, white or rosé) produced in the Burgundy region

Byrrh, sweet wine (fortified w/brandy) mixed w/quinine

Buche de
Nöel

cabécou, a strong, round goat cheese

Cabernet Sauvignon, dry red wine

cabillaud, cod

cabri, kid goat

cacahuète, peanut

cacao, cocoa

cachat, fresh cheese from Provence

Caen, à la mode de, cooked w/*calvados*

café, coffee (really, espresso)

café américain, American-style coffee

café au lait, coffee w/milk

café brûlot, flaming coffee
    (strong coffee w/liquor
    which is set on fire)

café complet, continental breakfast
    (coffee, bread, butter & jam)

café crème, coffee w/cream

café déca, decaffeinated coffee

café décaféiné, decaffeinated coffee

café de Paris, the name for a butter
    sauce flavored w/cognac & herbs

café espresso, espresso

café express, espresso

café filtre, drip-brewed coffee/
    American-style coffee

café frappé, iced coffee

café glacé, coffee-flavored ice
    cream/iced coffee

café liégeois, cold coffee
    served w/ice cream

café nature, black coffee

café noir, black coffee

café sans caféine, decaffeinated coffee

café soluble, instant coffee

café viennois, coffee w/whipped cream

cagouille, small land snail

cabri.

Cafe
Americain
also
Cafe ELongée
(AY-Lawn-Jay)
A large cup
of not-so-terribly
strong coffee.

Cafe Americain.

L'express.

You can
also ask
for coffee
"avec un petit
pot d'eau chaud..."
A small pot of
hot water to
dilute.

35

caille, quail

caillete, pâté of pork, herbs & garlic

calalou, "pepperpot" stew w/many
　　ingredients found in the French West Indies

calamar, squid

calissons, marzipan candies
　　shaped like boats from Aix

calmar, squid

calvados, apple brandy

camembert, soft cheese w/strong flavor

camomille, camomile tea

campagne, à la, this term means "country style" & has many
　　different meanings

canapé, appetizer w/bread base & topped w/various ingredients

canard, duck

canard à la presse, roast duck dish w/red wine & Cognac

canard à l'orange, roast duck braised w/orange sauce

canard de Barbarie, a duck breed in Southwest France

canard de Challans, a type of small duck

canard de Nantes, a type of small duck

canard de Rouen, a type of wild duck

canard laqué, Peking duck

canard Montmorency, duck w/cherries

canard rôti, roast duck

canard sauvage, wild duck

cancoillotte, strong, hard cheese (melted before serving) from
　　the Franche-Comté region in Eastern France

candi, candied

caneton, duckling

canette, young female duck

canistrelli, dry cookies from Corsica

cannelle, cinnamon

cantal, a cheese very much like cheddar

caouanne, turtle

capoun fassum, cabbage stuffed w/rice & sausage

câpre, caper

Caille
KA-EE

*Don't miss
Calalou if
you visit
Guadaloupe.*

Canard.

*Capoun Fassum...
like the sound
of that.*

36

caqhuse, pork & onion casserole

carafe, carafe

caramélisé, caramelized

caramel, burned sugar. This also refers to a chewy vanilla or chocolate caramel

carapaces, shells

carbonnade, braised beef stew (a Belgian specialty) also charcoal-grilled meat

carbonnade à la boeuf, Belgian specialty of beef marinated in beer & cooked in onions & herbs

carbonnade bruxelloise, Belgian dish of pork w/a tomato & tarragon sauce

carbonnade flamande, beef, herbs & onions braised in beer

carbonnade nîmoise, lamb & potato dish

cardinal, fish stock *velouté*, lobster butter & cream

cardomome, cardamom

cardon, cardoon (a member of the thistle family)

cargolade, grilled snail dish from Languedoc-Roussillon

carré d'agneau~
CAR-AY DON-YOH

cari, curry

carotte, carrot

carottes glacées, carrots glazed in butter

carottes râpées, grated carrots

carottes Vichy, steamed carrots (in butter & parsley)

carpe, carp

carré, rack /loin/fillet

carré d'agneau, rack or loin of lamb

carré de l'Est, pungent cheese (square shaped)

carré de porc, rack or loin of pork

carré de veau, rack or loin of veal

carrelet, flounder/plaice

carte, la, menu

carte des vins, wine list

carvi, caraway seeds

casse-croûte, snack ("breaking the crust")

casse-pierre, seaweed

carrelet.

cassis, black currant/black currant liqueur

cassolette, dish served in a small casserole

cassoulet (toulousain), meat & bean casserole. This dish originated in Southwest France

Cassoulet is one of man's greatest culinary achievements.

castagna, chestnut in Corsican

castanhet, chestnut cake

cavaillon, a fragrant melon from the town of the same name in Provence. It looks like a small cantaloupe

cave, wine shop/wine cellar

caviar, fish eggs

caviar d'aubergine, eggplant purée

cédrat, citron

céleri, celery

céleri-rave, celery root

céleri rémoulade, celery root in a creamy mayonnaise dressing

cendre chemisée, smoldering

cèpe, boletus mushroom

céréale, cereal

cerf, venison (deer)

cerfeuil, chervil

cerise, cherry

Cerises.

cerise noire, black cherry

cerises jubilé, cherries flamed w/*kirsch* & served w/ice cream

cerneau, the "meat" of a walnut

cervelas, seasoned sausage made from brains

cervelle, brain

cervelle de canut, herbed cheese spread from Lyon

cervelles, brains *You've been warned.*

chabichou, cow's- & goat's-milk cheese. Some think it has a sweet flavor

Chablis, one of France's wine regions producing white wine made from the chardonnay grape

chair, "fleshy" part of fish or meat

Challonaise, wine region producing mostly table wine

chambré, room temperature (when serving wine)

Champagne, A region in Northeastern France famous
for its sparkling wines classified by the sugar content.
Brut is the driest, ***extra-sec*** is very dry, ***sec*** is
dry, ***demi-sec*** is slightly sweet & ***doux*** is sweet.
Also a sweet cookie served w/champagne

champenoise, sparkling wine

champêtre, this term means "rustic" & can
mean many things. Usually this term
means a simple dish

Champignons.

champignon, mushroom

champignon à la grecque, cold mushroom appetizer

champignon de bois, wild mushroom

champignon de Paris, button mushroom

champignon de pin, pine mushroom. A wild mushroom found
in Provence

champignon sauvage, wild mushroom

changement de garniture, this means an extra charge for
substitutions

chansons aux pommes, flaky breakfast pastry w/apple filling

chanterelle, chanterelle mushroom

chantilly, sweet whipped cream. This can also refer to
hollandaise sauce & whipped cream

chaource, cheese found in the Champagne region

chapelure, breadcrumbs

chapon, capon

Chantilly ~
Shan-tee-ee

chapon de mer, scorpion fish

charbonnade, charcoal-grilled meat

charcuterie, can be a deli or any
place serving prepared meats.
This can also refer to cooked pork meats

charcuterie assortie, assorted cold meats

chariot, dessert &/or cheese cart

charlotte, fruit dessert made in a mold/baked fruit
compote/pudding

charolais, denotes a high-quality beef

chartreuse, yellow (or green) herb liqueur. Also a game bird
    (usually pheasant or partridge) dish from Alsace

chasse, venison

chasselas, a white grape

chasseur, "hunter's style" usually means in a sauce w/tomatoes,
    wine, herbs & mushrooms

châtaigne, chestnut

châtaignes chaudes/marrons chauds, roasted chestnuts

chateaubriand, thick slice of tenderloin stuffed w/sauteed
    shallots & usually served w/butter or *béarnaise* sauce

Château-Margaux, red wine from Bordeaux

Châteauneuf-du-Pape, red wine from the Rhône River valley

chaud, hot

chaud-froid, cold poultry dish/a dish containing gelatin. It's
    cooked & then served cold, thus the name which means
    "hot-cold"

chaud ~ show
froid ~ fwa

chaudrée, seafood & fish stew
    (contains the white part of squid)

chauffé, heated

chaumes, rich, creamy cheese from Dordogne

chausson, fruit turnover

chausson aux pommes, apple turnover

chemise, en, baked in parchment/wrapped in pastry

cheval, horse

chèvre, goat/goat cheese

chevreau, young goat

cheval, it's still eaten in France.

chèvre fraîche, goat cheese which is only a few days old

chèvre seche, dried (aged) goat cheese

chevreuil, deer

chichi, orange-flavored doughnuts

chevreuil ~ chev-ray

chicorée, chicory/endive

chicorée frisée, curly lettuce

chicorée witloof, Belgian endive

chiffonnade, shredded leafy vegetables & herbs

chinchard, saurel, a fish

chinois, Chinese

Chinon, red wine from the Loire Valley

chipiron, small squid

chipirons en su tinta, Basque dish of squid
cooked in its own ink

chipolatas, small sausages

chips, potato chips

chivry, a *béarnaise* sauce w/spinach, parsley or watercress
added to make it green

chocolat, chocolate

chocolat à la bayonne, chocolate cream dessert

chocolat amer, bitter chocolate

chocolat au lait, milk chocolate

chocolat chaud, hot chocolate

chocolat mi-amer, bittersweet chocolate

chocolat noir, bitter chocolate/black chocolate

choix, "choice." On a menu, this means you can choose among
a list of dishes

chope, large beer

choron, *béarnaise* sauce w/tomatoes

chou, cabbage

chou à la crème, cream puff

choucroute, sauerkraut. In Alsace, this refers to a dish of
cabbage w/pork, potatoes & sauerkraut

choucroute garnie, sauerkraut w/ham, *Love this!*
pork sausage or frankfurters

chouée, buttered cabbage dish

chou-fleur, cauliflower

chou frisé, kale/savoy cabbage

chou marin, kale

chou rouge, red cabbage

chou vert, green cabbage

choux de Bruxelles, brussels sprouts

ciboule, scallion

ciboulette, chive

cidre, cider. Popular in Brittany

cigales, a type of clam

*In Brittany
you must
drink cider
with your
crepes &
galettes.*

cigarette, sugar cookie (rolled in the shape of a cigarette)

citron, the term for lemons & limes (citrus fruit) but can also simply refer to a lemon

citronelle, lemon grass

citronnade, lemon drink

citron pressé, fresh lemon juice w/sugar & water (lemonade)

citron vert, lime

citrouille, pumpkin

civelles, baby eels

civet, game stew. Popular in Corsica

civet de lapin, rabbit stew

civet de lièvre, hare stew

Essentially the same thing

clafouti, fruit baked in pancake batter

clafouti du limousin, cherry *clafouti*

Love clafouti!

claires, oysters (raised in an oyster bed)

clamart, stuffed w/green peas

Claret, dry, red table wine from Bordeaux

clémentine, seedless tangerine

clos, vineyard

clou de girofle, clove

clouté, "studded with"

cocaos, cocoa

cochon, pig

cochon de lait, suckling pig

Cochon.

cochon de lait en gelée, suckling pig in aspic. A specialty in Luxembourg

cochonnailles, assorted pork sausages & pâtés

cocotte, casserole

coeur, heart

coeur d'artichaut, artichoke heart

coeur de filet, thickest & best part of a beef filet

coeurs de palmiers, hearts of palm served w/a mustard vinaigrette

coeur d'artichaut ~ Kerr Part-e-show

cognac, cognac

coing, quince

Cointreau, orange-flavored liqueur

colbert, à la, dipped in batter & breadcrumbs & fried
colin, hake
colonel, lemon sherbet w/vodka
colvert, wild duck
complet, full/whole
compote, stewed fruit
compote de..., stewed
compris, included 
comté, a mild cheese (similar to the Swiss gruyère cheese)
concassé, chopped
concentré, concentrate
concombre, cucumber
concorde, chocolate meringue & chocolate mousse
condiments, seasoning
confiserie, candy & sweets shop
confit, goose, pork, turkey or duck preserved in fat
　　Also vegetables/fruit preserved in alcohol, sugar or vinegar
confiture, jam/preserves.
　　Confiture d'oignons is onion compote
confiture de vieux garçon, fruit served in alcohol
confiture d' orange, marmalade
congre, conger eel
consommation, drinks
consommé, broth (clear soup)
consommé aux vermicelles, broth w/thin noodles
consommé Célestine, broth w/chicken & noodles
consommé colbert, broth w/vegetables & poached eggs
consommé madrilène, cold broth w/tomatoes
consommé princesse, broth w/chicken & asparagus
consultez aussi l'ardoise, other suggestions
　　on the blackboard
consultez notre carte des desserts, consult our dessert menu
contre-filet, sirloin
copeaux, shavings (of vegetables or chocolate)
copieux, filling
coppa, fillet (in Corsica)

[handwritten note: Concombre. (with drawing of cucumber)]

[handwritten note: Confiture de coco is coconut preserves served in the West Indies. Love it!]

43

coq, rooster

coq au vin, chicken stewed in red wine
w/bacon, onions, mushrooms & herbs

coq de bruyère, grouse

coque, tiny shellfish (similar to a clam)

coquelet, cockerel

coquillage, shellfish

coquille, shell/scallop

coquille Saint-Jacques, scallop (prepared w/a
parsley butter or a cream sauce)

coquilles à la nantaise, scallops w/onions.
A specialty in Brittany

corail, the egg sac of lobster,
crayfish or scallops

corbeille, basket

corbeille de fruits, basket of assorted fruits

cordon bleu, veal slices stuffed w/ham &
gruyere, breaded & fried in butter

coriandre, coriander

cornet de frites, paper cone filled
w/french fries. A popular snack

cornets de murat, cones filled w/cream

cornichon, small pickle (gherkin)

corniottes, cheese pastry made in the shape of hats

corps, refers to the "body" of wine

corsoise, à la, this means that the dish is prepared
as it would in Corsica

cosse, pod/husk

côte, rib/chop

côte d'agneau, lamb chop

Côte de Beaune, red & white wines from Beaune in Burgundy

côte de boeuf, beef rib steak/T-bone steak

Côte de Nuits, a heavy red Burgundy wine

côte de veau, veal chop

côtelette, cutlet/chop

côtelette d'agneau, lamb chop

Le Coq.
The Symbol
of France.
Not too smart.
Lot's of noise.
Can't fly.
Makes you think

Côte de Beaune.
one of our
favorite wines.

44

côtelette de porc, pork chop

Côtes du Rhône, wine region producing wines such as
Châteauneuf-du-Pape, Côte-Rotie, Hermitage & Tavel

côtes levées, spareribs

cotignac, caramelized apple tart

cotriade, fish stew (from Brittany)

cou, neck

cou d'oie farci, a "sausage" made of the neck skin of a goose
which is stuffed w/meat & spices

couennes de porc, fresh pork rinds

coulibiac, salmon *pâté*

coulis, vegetable, shellfish or fruit purée

coulis de tomates, thick tomato sauce

coulommiers, a mild cheese (similar to *brie*)

coupe, goblet/scoop/a dish used for serving dessert

coupe Danemark, a scoop of vanilla ice cream covered w/hot
chocolate sauce

coupe des îles, a scoop of vanilla ice cream w/fruit & whipped
cream

Courgettes.

coupe glacée, ice cream dessert (often a sundae)

courge, squash

courgette, zucchini

courgettes au broccio, *broccio* cheese stuffed
zucchini dish from Corsica

couronne, circle-shaped or ring-shaped bread

court bouillon, seafood broth

couscous, Moroccan specialty of steamed grain, broth, meats,
vegetables & other ingredients

couscous royal, *couscous* w/meat

cousinat, bean, bell pepper, artichoke, tomato, green onion &
carrot dish

couteau, knife

Couteau.

couvert, cover charge

couvert, vin et service compris, the price includes wine,
tip & cover charge

crabe, crab

crabe verte, shore crab

crapaudine, grilled game or poultry dish

craquelins, cookies

Crécy, à la, served w/carrots

crème, cream/creamy soup/creamy dessert. Can also refer to
 sweet liqueur as in *crème de menthe*. *À la crème* means
 served w/a cream sauce

crème à la vanille, vanilla custard

crème allégée, light cream

crème anglaise, custard

crème brûlée, custard dessert topped w/caramelized sugar

crème caramel, vanilla custard w/caramel sauce

crème catalane, caramel-covered trifle w/cinnamon & anise

crème champignons, cream of mushroom soup

crème chantilly, vanilla-flavored & sweetened whipped cream

crème d'asperges, cream of asparagus soup

crème de cacao, cocoa-flavored liqueur

crème de cassis, black currant liqueur

crème de marrons, chestnut purée

crème de menthe, mint-flavored liqueur

crème de poireaux, cream of leek soup

crème de poulet, cream of chicken soup

crème de volaille, cream of chicken soup

crème épaisse, heavy cream

crème fouettée, whipped cream

crème fraîche, thick, heavy cream

crème frit, fried cream custard dessert from Burgundy

crème glacée, ice cream

crème pâtissière, custard filling in cakes & pastry

crème plombières, custard filled w/fresh fruit

crème renversée, custard dessert in a mold

crèmerie, store selling dairy products

cremets, cream made in molds w/fruit

crêpe, crepe (thin pancake). Popular in Brittany

crêpe froment, buckwheat crepe w/sweet filling

crêpe Suzette, crepe w/orange sauce, flamed w/orange liqueur

*Anything
"Crème" is
OK by us.*

crépine, caul fat (fat covering the intestines) used to wrap *pâtés & terrines*

I didn't need to know this.

crépinette, small sausage patty wrapped in caul fat

cresson, watercress

cressonade, watercress sauce

cressonière, watercress soup

crête de coq, cock's comb (the fleshy crest on the head of fowl)

creuse, a type of oyster

crevette, shrimp

crevette grise, gray, small shrimp

crevette rose, red shrimp w/firm flesh

cristallisés, crystallized

crist-marine, algae

croissant, crescent-shaped flaky breakfast roll made of flour, eggs & butter

If you're looking up croissant you're really in trouble!

croquant, crispy

croquants, crispy honey or almond cookies

croque madame, toasted ham & cheese sandwich topped w/an egg

croquemboche, cream-puff tree

Croque monsieur. Love these.

croque monsieur, toasted ham & cheese sandwich

croquette, ground meat, fish or vegetables coated in bread crumbs & deep fried

crosse, shank

crottin/croutin de chavignol, a firm goat cheese

croustade, pie filled w/meat, seafood &/or vegetables

croustillant, crisp/spicy

croûte, crust

croûte au fromage, melted cheese served on a slice of toast

croûte de sel, en, in a salt crust

croûte, en, in a pastry crust

croûte forestière, mushrooms on toast

Yes, please!

croûtes, croutons

croûton, small toasted piece of bread, usually served in a salad

cru, raw. On a wine list, this means vintage

cru classé, high-quality wine

crudités, raw vegetables

crustacé, shellfish (crustaceans)

cuiller, spoon

cuillère, à la, a dish eaten w/a spoon

cuisine, there are four categories of French cuisine:

Cuisine campagnarde (also known as *cuisine des provinces*):
Traditional regional dishes prepared with fresh ingredients.

Cuisine bourgeoise: French home cooking.

Haute cuisine: An elaborate meal with many courses featuring
rich and fresh ingredients.

Nouvelle cuisine: Light sauces and small portions which
emphasize the colors and textures of the ingredients.

cuisse, leg & thigh (denotes dark meat)

cuisse de poulet, chicken drumstick w/thigh

cuisses de grenouilles, frogs' legs

cuissot, haunch of game or veal

cuit, cooked

cuit à la vapeur, steamed

cuit au four, baked

cul, haunch

cul de veau, veal pot roast

culotte, rump

cumin, cumin

curaçao, orange-flavored liqueur

curcuma, the spice tumeric (used in curry powder)

cure-dent, (served w/a) toothpick

currie/curry, curry

cuvée, blend of wines or champagne/house wine

Cynar, aperitif w/an artichoke base

darne, thick fillet of fish (often salmon)

dartois, pastry w/jam

datte, date

daube, stew

daube à la niçoise, beef or lamb stew w/red wine, tomatoes &
onions

[handwritten note: Cuisse, the dark meat of poultry is the more prized meat in France.]

[handwritten note: cuit ~ cwee]

48

daube de boeuf, beef stew

daube provençal, gravy w/capers, garlic & anchovies

dauphinois, a mild cheese

daurade, white fish (usually served grilled) found in the South of France (sea bream)

déca, decaf

décafféiné, decaffeinated

décortiqué, shelled/peeled

déglacée, warmed up

dégustation, sampling/tasting

déjeuner, lunch

délice, a delight/a treat

You can order just "Deca" "De-CAH" Decaf.

délimité de qualité supérieure, on a wine bottle, this means a superior-quality wine

demi, half/small beer

demi-bouteille, half bottle

demi-deuil, usually means served w/truffles

demidoff, w/vegetables

demi-glace, beef-stock sauce

demi-sel, soft, salty cream cheese

demi-sec, medium dry

demoiselle de Cherbourg, small lobster

denté, dentex (fish)

désossé, boned

dessert, dessert

diable, hot, spicy sauce (often, a strong mustard sauce)/ devilled. This is also the term for an unglazed, porous pot used to cook vegetables

diabolo, a drink usually mixed w/lemonade

diane, a brown sauce w/vinegar & peppercorns

dieppoise, shrimp & mussels served in a white wine sauce

digestif, after-dinner drink

dijonnaise, served w/mustard

dinde, turkey

dindon, turkey

dindonneau, young turkey

Dinde.

dîner, dinner

diplomate, custard dessert w/spongecake, crystallized fruit & topped w/liqueur

discrétion, when you see this on a menu, it means that you can drink as much wine as you want (for a fixed price)

Our experience has been that when you may drink as much wine as you wish, the wine isn't exactly the best.

divine, *hollandaise* sauce w/sherry

dodine de canard, stuffed-duck dish

domaine, on a wine label this notes a high-quality wine

dorade, Mediterranean sea bass

doré(e), golden

dos, back

dos et ventre, both sides (means "back & front")

douce, sweet

doucette, salad green (a cousin of *mâche*)

douceurs, desserts

doux, mild, sweet

douzaine, dozen

dragées, candied almonds

Dubonnet, wine & brandy-based aperitif w/herbs

duchesse, potatoes mixed w/egg & forced through a pastry tube

dugléré, a white sauce w/tomatoes, shallots & white wine

duxelles, finely chopped sautéed mushrooms

eau, water

eau au syphon, w/seltzer water

eau avec gaz, carbonated water

eau de source, spring water

You may ask for "un verre d'eau" - a glass of water or simply "de l'eau" (duh Low)

eau-de-vie, brandy made from distilled fruit juice. Sold in elaborate tall & thin bottles in Alsace. The term means "water of life." This can also refer to any spirit

eau du robinet, tap water

eau glacée, iced water

eau minérale, mineral water

eau minérale gazeuse, carbonated mineral water

eau nature, tap water

eau plate, still (not sparkling) water

eau sans gaz, water w/out carbonation

ecailler, oyster opener/fish scaler

échalote, shallot

échine, spareribs

éclair, pastry filled w/vanilla custard & topped w/chocolate icing

écrevisse, crayfish

écrevisse à la nage, crayfish in a white wine sauce

édam français, nutty-flavored, orange-colored cheese originally from the Netherlands

édulcorant, artificial sweetener

effilées, thinly sliced

effiloché, thinly sliced

églefin, haddock

emballé, wrapped

emballage is packaging

embeurré, buttered/buttery

embeurrée de chou, buttered cabbage

émincé, slices of cooked meat in gravy/thinly sliced

émincé de veau, sauteed veal slices w/creme sauce

emmental, Swiss cheese

emporter, à, take-out foods

émulsionné, liquified

Endive. George Bush knows how to pronounce this correctly.

enchaud de porc à la périgourdine, pork loin stuffed w/truffles. A specialty in Southwest France

encornet, small squid

endive, endive/chicory

enrubanne, layered dish (looks like ribbons)

Enchaud de porc à la Perigourdine if you see this on a menu, go for it!

entier, whole

entrecôte, rib-eye steak

entrecôte Bercy, steak w/wine sauce

entrecôte maître d'hôtel, rib-eye steak served w/herb butter

entrecôte marchand de vin, rib-eye steak served in
  red wine sauce
Entre-Deux-Mers, a region of Bordeaux
  which produces white wine
entrée, first course/appetizer
entremets, dessert
épaule, shoulder
épeautre, a variety of wheat
éperlan, smelt
épice, spice
épicé, peppered/spicy
épicerie, small grocery store
épi de maïs, miniature corn
  on the cob (often pickled)
épinard, spinach
épinards en branches, leaf spinach
époisse, a cow's-milk cheese from Burgundy
érable, maple
escabèche, raw fish marinated in lime juice & herbs. In
  Provence, this can also refer to a cold marinated sardine
  dish
escalope, scallop/cutlet
escalope de veau, veal scallop
escalope panée, breaded veal scallop
escalope viennoise, breaded veal cutlet (weiner schnitzel)
escargot, snail
escargot de mer, sea snail
escargot petit-gris, small snail
escarole, a type of *endive*
espadon, swordfish
essence, essence
estocaficada, cod stew
estofat de boeuf, beef stew
estouffade, beef stew. Can also refer to a steamed dish
estouffados, almond butter cookies found in Provence
estragon, tarragon

Watch out... Unlike in the U.S. the entrée is the first course not the main course.

We love going in small grocery stores.

Escargot.

esturgeon, sturgeon
et, and
étrille, small crab
étouffée, stewed
étuvé/étuvée, steamed
éventail, en, cut into a fan shape
express, espresso
extra-sec, very dry (champagne)
façon, in the manner of
faisan, pheasant
faisan normand, pheasant w/apples & *calvados*
faisselle, fresh cow's-milk cheese
fait à la maison, homemade
falette, stuffed breast of veal
far, prune tart
farandole, dessert &/or cheese cart
farce, spiced ground meat (usually pork) used for stuffing
farci, stuffed, as in *chou farci* (stuffed cabbage) & *tomates farcies* (stuffed tomatoes). In Nice, this is a dish of stuffed vegetables
farigoule, the name in Provence for wild thyme
farine, flour
farine de blé, wheat flour
farine de maïs, corn flour
faux-filet, flank steak/sirloin steak
fécule, starch. *Fécule de pommes de terre* is potato flour used to thicken sauces & soups
fécule de maïs, cornstarch
fendant, "melting." Refers to extremely tender meat or chocolate
fenouil, fennel
féra, the fish dace (lake salmon)
ferme, farm/farm fresh
fermier, poultry raised on a farm
feu de bois, cooked on a wood fire
feuille, leaf

[handwritten note: faison is common during the hunt season in the fall.]

[handwritten note: feuille ~ Foy·ee]

feuille de chêne, oak-leaf lettuce
feuille de laurel, bay leaf
feuille de vigne, vine leaf
feuilles farcies, grape leaves stuffed w/rice & herbs
feuilletage, puff pastry
feuilletée, puff pastry
fève, broad bean
fiadone, cheesecake found in Corsica
ficelle, small baguette. *Ficellé* means tied w/a string
figatelli, Corsican liver sausage
figue, fig
figue de barbarie, prickly pear
filet, fillet
filet à la mistral, filet of sole w/tomatoes & mushrooms
filet de boeuf, beef fillet
filet de boeuf à la Poitou, beef fillet w/chicken liver *pâté*
filet de boeuf Bordelaise, beef fillet in a red wine sauce
filet de sole, fillet of sole
filet de sole meunière, fillet of sole fried in butter
filet doria, fillet of sole w/cucumbers
filet mignon, small round meat fillet
filet Saint-Germain, fillet of sole w/potatoes
financière, cream & Madeira wine sauce. This can also refer to
    a dish w/veal or chicken dumplings
fine, a fine brandy
fines de claire, oysters
fines herbes, mixture of herbs (such as parsley, chives, tarragon
    & thyme)
flageolets, small kidney-shaped beans
flagnarde/flaugnarde, fruit-filled cake
flamande, à la, "Flemish style" w/potatoes, stuffed cabbage
    leaves, vegetables, sausage & bacon
flambé(e), flaming
flamiche, savory tart (similar to a quiche)
flan, tart or crustless pie. Can also refer to the caramel custard
    dessert of the same name found in Spain

*fines herbes -
Feen-zerb*

flanchet, flank
flet, flounder
flétan, halibut

(handwritten note: "fleur." with a small drawing)

fleur, flower. *Fleurs* are crystallized flowers used on desserts
fleurette, small flower
Fleurie, a red wine from Beaujolais
fleurons, crescent-shaped puff pastries
fleurs de courgette farcies, zucchini flowers stuffed w/cheese
flocon, flake
flocons d'avoine, oat flakes
florentine, w/spinach
foie, liver
foie de veau, calf's liver
foie de veau grand-mère, sautéed calf's liver w/bacon,
    onion & potato garnish
foie de volaille, chicken liver
foie gras, fattened goose liver
foie gras de canard, fattened duck liver
foie gras d'oie, fattened goose liver
foie gras en brioche, fattened goose liver that is marinated &
    cooked & baked a second time in a pastry shell
foies blonds de volaille, chicken livers
foin, cooked in hay *(handwritten note: "Huh?")*
fond, bottom
fondant, cake icing
fondant au chocolate, similar to a brownie (but better!)
fond d'artichaut, artichoke heart
fondu/fondue (au fromage), melted cheese in a pot. Dip your
    bread or meat in!
fondu aux raisins, the crust of this smooth & creamy cheese is
    made of grape pulp. Also known as *tomme au marc*
fondue bourguignonne, small pieces of meat dipped into
    oil & eaten w/sauces
fondue chinoise, thin slices of beef dipped in bouillon
    & eaten w/sauces
fondue Savoyarde, pot of melted cheese for dipping

forestière, ("forester's style") usually means w/sautéed mushrooms

forêt noire, Black Forest cake

forme d'Ambert, a blue cheese

formule, une, a set-price menu

fort, strong (as in strong or sharp cheese)

fougasse, decorated bread loaf w/olive oil flavoring & sometimes w/bacon, onion or tomato stuffing

fougassette, a slice of broiche bread flavored w/orange & saffron

four, au, baked

fourchette, fork

fournée, baked

fournitures, fresh herbs & salad greens

fourré, filled/stuffed

fraîche, fresh

frais, fresh

fraise, strawberry

fraise des bois, wild strawberry

framboise, raspberry/raspberry liqueur

frangipane, almond custard filling

frappé, drink blended w/ice

frémis, oysters (served almost raw)

friand, meat-filled pastry

friandises, *petits fours*

fricadelles, fried meat patties *Love these!*

fricadelles à la bière, meatballs in beer. A specialty in Belgium

fricandeau, braised veal dish

fricassée, a stew of meat, poultry or fish finished w/cream

fricassée liégeoise, fried eggs, bacon & sausage. A specialty in Belgium

frigolet, name in Provence for wild thyme

frisée, curly endive

frit, fried

fritelli, chestnut-flour doughnuts from Corsica

frites, french fries (often eaten w/mayonnaise)

fraise .

fritons, minced spread made of organ meats

Fritons...
I'll pass.

fritot, batter fried or fritter

friture, frying

friture de mer/friture de poisson, fried small fish

froid, cold

fromage, cheese. It is said that there are over 400 different
French cheeses

fromage à pâte dure, hard cheese

fromage à pâte molle, soft cheese

fromage au marc, a sharp, tangy cheese

fromage blanc, cream cheese (but runny)

fromage de brebis, sheep's-milk cheese

fromage de chèvre, goat's-milk cheese

fromage de tête, headcheese (sausage made from the meat of a
calf's or pig's head which is cooked in a gelatinous meat
broth & then served cold)

fromage fermier, cheese made where the milk is produced

fromage fort, extremely soft cheese from Provence mixed
w/herbs, salt, pepper & *marc*

fromage maigre, low-fat cheese

fromagerie, cheese shop

fruit, fruit

fruit confit, candied fruit

fruit de la passion, passion fruit

fruits de mer, seafood

fumé, smoked

fumet, fish stock

Galantine.
Pass on this too.

galantine, cold gelatinized meat dish

galette, buckwheat pancake/tart

galette bretonne, butter & rum cake

galette de pommes, apple tart

galette de sarrasin, buckwheat pancake w/savoury filling
popular in Brittany

galopin, bread pancake   *Love this word*

Gamay de Touraine, red wine made w/the Gamay grape

gambas, large prawns

gambas à la planxa, grilled shrimp served on a plank of wood

ganses, fried cakes topped w/sugar

garbure, cabbage soup. In Southern France, this is usually cabbage soup w/ham

garni(e), w/vegetables/garnished

garniture, vegetables/garnished

gâteau, cake

gâteau au chocolat, chocolate cake

gâteau au fromage, cheese tart

gâteau de Savoie, spongecake

gâteau de riz, rice pudding

gateau.

gaufre, waffle. A specialty in Belgium

gaufrette, sweet wafer

gayettes, small sausage patties

gazeuse, carbonated. *Non-gazeuse* means not carbonated

gelé, frozen

gelée, jellied/in aspic

gélinotte, prairie chicken

genièvre, juniper berry

génoise, spongecake

germiny, sorrel & cream soup/w/sorrel

gésier, gizzard

Gewürztraminer, dry white wine from Alsace

gibelotte de lapin, rabbit stew

gibier, game

gigot, leg

gigot d'agneau, leg of lamb

gigot d'agneau~

Gee-go dan Yott

gigot de mer, oven-roasted monkfish dish

gigot de mouton pré-salé, leg of lamb dish made w/lambs that graze in salt meadows in Northwest France

gigot farci, stuffed leg of lamb

gigue, the haunch of game meat

gimblettes, ring cookies

gin, gin

gingembre, ginger

gin tonique, gin & tonic

girofle, clove
girolle, chanterelle mushroom 
glaçage, frosting
glace, ice/ice cream
glacé, iced/glazed

glaçons (handwritten note)

glace à la napolitaine, layers of different flavored ice cream
glace au fondant, shiny cake icing
glace crémeuse, ice cream
glace de viande, concentrated meat stock (meat glaze)
glace de poisson, concentrated fish stock
glaçons, ice
globe, round (cut of meat)
gnocchi, gnocchi (potato dumplings). Found frequently on
   menus in Nice & near the Italian border
gnocchi aux blettes, gnocchi w/Swiss chard
   incorporated into the dough
gougere, cheese-flavored pastry
goujon, gudgeon (related to carp)
goujonnettes, small slices of fish
gourmandises, sweets/candies
gousse, clove
gousse d'ail, clove of garlic
goûter, snack
graine, grain/seed
graine de maïs, corn meal
graine de moutarde, mustard seed
graines de paradis, similar to the spice cardamom & found in
   the former French African colonies
graisse, fat
graisserons, fried pieces of goose or duck skin
grand, large
grand crème, a large milky coffee
grand cru, high-quality wine
Grand Marnier, orange liqueur
grand-mère, means "grandmother." A garnish usually of
   mushrooms, potatoes & bacon

Gougere is traditionally made with gruyere cheese. (handwritten note)

gouter means to taste (handwritten note)

grand veneur, brown sauce w/red currants (usually served w/game)

grand vin, high-quality wine

granité, slushy iced drink

gras, fat/fatty

gras-double, tripe simmered in wine & onions

Gras-double... we'll pass...

gratin, au, topped w/grated cheese, breadcrumbs & butter & then baked

gratin dauphinois, potato au gratin dish w/eggs, cheese & cream

gratin de fruits de mer, shellfish in a cream sauce

gratin de queues d'écrevisses, freshwater crayfish served *au gratin*

gratin de capucins, *gratin* of stuffed artichoke hearts

gratin savoyard, baked sliced-potato casserole

gratiné, prepared w/breadcrumbs

gratinée, topped w/cheese/onion soup

grattons, fried pieces of pork, goose or duck skin

gratuit, free

Graves, wine region of Bordeaux

grecque, cold vegetable mixture (*légumes à la grecque*). *À la grecque* refers to dishes stewed in oil (in the Greek style)

grelot, small white onion

grenade, pomegranate

grenadin, small veal scallop

grenoblois, caramel-walnut cake

grenouille, frog

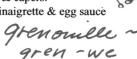

grenouille ~ gren-we

gribiche, mayonnaise w/*cornichons* & capers. *Sauce gribich*e can refer to a vinaigrette & egg sauce

grillade, grilled meat/mixed grill

grillé, grilled

griotte, a type of cherry (usually in white alcohol)

grive, thrush (a bird)

grondin, spiked-headed ocean fish (gurnet)

gros bout de poitrine, brisket

groseille, currant

groseille à maquereau, gooseberry/currant

groseille rouge, red currant

gros sel, coarse salt

grumes, heavy coating or skin

gruyère, Swiss cheese

guimauve, marshmallow

haché, hashed

hachis, hash

hachis parmentier, shepherd's pie (ground meat & mashed
   potatoes topped w/a white sauce & served in a casserole)

hareng, herring

harengs fumés à la Créole, spicy smoked herring dish flamed
   in rum (found in the French West Indies)

haricot, bean

haricot de mer, tiny clam

haricot de mouton, mutton, bean
   & potato stew

haricot de soisson, navy bean/kidney bean

haricot rouge, red kidney bean

haricots en salade, bean salad

haricots verts, green beans (french beans)

Henri IV, artichoke hearts & *béarnaise* sauce

herbes, herbs

herbes de Provence, mixture of herbs that includes fennel,
   lavender, marjoram, bay leaf, sage, rosemary & thyme

hérisson de mer, sea urchin

hochepot, oxtail stew

hollandaise, sauce of melted butter, egg yolks & lemon juice

homard, lobster

homard à l'américaine, flaming lobster dish w/white wine,
   herbs, tomatoes & garlic

homard à l'armoricaine, lobster in a tomato sauce

homard cardinal, flaming lobster dish w/mushrooms & truffles

homard froid à la parisienne, cold lobster garnished w/diced
   vegetables in a mayonnaise sauce

haricots.

haricots verts.

homard Newburg, lobster cooked in a sauce made of butter, cream, wine (or brandy) & egg yolks

homard Thermidor, flaming lobster dish w/white wine, herbs, spices & mustard

hongroise, served w/paprika & cream (means "Hungarian")

hors d'oeuvre, appetizer

huile, oil

huile d'arachide, peanut oil

huile de carthame, safflower oil

huile de noix, walnut oil

huile de soya, soybean oil

huile de tournesol, sunflower oil

huile d'olive (vierge), olive oil (virgin)

huître, oyster

huître belon, pink oyster

huître portugaise, Portuguese lobster (small & fat)

hure de porc, pig's head

hure de saumon, salmon pâté

hysope, the bitter herb hysop

île flottante, meringues floating in a cream sauce

impératrice, rice-pudding dessert

importée, imported

indienne, w/curry (in the style of India)

infusion, herbal tea

jalousies, apricot pastry

jambe, leg

jambon, ham

jambon à l'os, baked ham

jambon blanc, boned, cooked ham

jambon cuit, cooked ham

jambon cuit d'Ardennes, smoked ham found in Belgium

jambon de Bayonne, raw, salty ham

jambon de canard, cured, salted or smoked duck or goose breast

jambon de montagne, local cured ham

Homard.

île flottante means floating island.

os means bone.

62

jambon de Paris, lightly salted ham
jambon de Parme, Parma ham (prosciutto)
jambon de pays, local "country" cured ham
jambon de York, smoked ham (English style)
jambon d'oie, cured, salted or smoked duck or goose breast
jambon cru, cured ham
jambonneau, pork knuckle
jambon persillé, parsleyed ham
jardinière, w/diced vegetables
jarret, shank/knuckle
jarret de veau, veal shank
    (usually a stew)
jerez, sherry (spanish for sherry)
Jésus de Morteau, smoked pork sausage
jeune, young/green (as in unripe)
joue, cheek
jour, du, of the day
jud mat gardebóneh, smoked pork &
    bean dish found in Luxembourg
julienne, vegetables cut into fine strips.
    There is also a fish w/this name
jumeau, pot roast
Jura, one of France's wine-growing regions
jus, juice/gravy
jus de tomate, tomato juice
jus d'orange, orange juice
kaki, persimmon
kalouga, chocolate-pudding cake
ketchup, ketchup
kig-ha-farz, buckwheat pudding
    w/vegetables & meat
kir, apéritif made w/*crème de cassis* & wine
kir royal, apéritif made w/champagne & *crème de cassis*
kirsch, cherry-flavored liqueur
kougelhopf/kouglof/kugelhopf, Alsacian cake w/raisins
    & almonds

jambon persillé is generally shredded & served in jelly and frankly it's not up our alley.

jus d'orange is frequently served with water & packets of sugar.

If you're looking this up you've had too much to drink.

kouigh amann, buttered pastry

l', la, le, the (singular). *Les* is the (plural)

lait, milk

laitance, fish roe

lait de beurre, buttermilk

lait écrémé, skim milk

lait entier, whole milk

laitue, lettuce

lambi, conch found in the French West Indies

lamelle, very thin slice

lamproie, lamprey

lamproie... no merci

langouste, crayfish

langouste à la sètoise, lobster (crawfish) w/garlic, tomatoes &
     cognac

langoustine, prawn

langue, tongue

langue de chat, biscuit & ice-cream dessert

Languedoc, one of France's wine-growing regions

languedocienne, usually means eggplant,
     tomato & mushroom garnish

lapereau, young rabbit

lapin.

lapin, rabbit

lapin à l'artésienne, rabbit stew

lapin à la Lorraine, rabbit in a mushroom & cream sauce

lapin aux pruneaux, rabbit w/prunes. A popular dish in
     Northern France

lapin chasseur, rabbit in a white wine & herb sauce

lapin de garenne, wild rabbit

lapin en paquets, rabbit pieces in a packet
     of bacon. A specialty in Provence

Lavender is also added to Herbes de Provence.

lard, bacon

lardon, diced bacon

laurier, bay leaf

lavande, lavender. Lavender blossoms are added to dishes in
     Provence such as *sorbet de lavande* (lavender sorbet)

lèche, thin slice (usually of meat or bread)

léger, light

légère, light (as in light beer)

légumes, vegetables

lentilles, lentils

levraut, young rabbit

levure, yeast

libre service, self-service

lieu, small saltwater fish

lièvre, rabbit (hare)

lièvre en cabessal, stuffed hare dish

limande, dab (flounder)

limande sole, lemon sole

limonade, lemonade

liqueur, liqueur

lisette, small mackerel

lit, bed (as in a bed of lettuce)

Lotte.

litre, liter. Wine is often served in a liter carafe, *demi-litre* (half liter) or *un quart* (quarter-liter)

livarot, round, sharp, tangy cheese

Loire, this valley is one of France's wine regions along the Loire River

longe, loin

longe de veau, loin of veal

longeole, pork sausage stuffed w/cabbage, leeks & spinach. A specialty in French-speaking Switzerland

lonzu, shoulder (in Corsica)

lorraine, usually braised in red wine w/cabbage

lotte, monkfish

loubine, fish similar to sea bass

lou cachat, crushed cheese

lou magret, breast of fattened goose or duck

lou mäis, corn meal cake found in Provence

"lou" is provencal for "the"

loup, sea bass

loup aux fenouille, sea bass grilled over fennel stalks

loup de mer, sea bass

lou pevre, goat's-milk cheese w/coarsely ground pepper

lou piech, stuffed veal dish found around Nice

louvine, fish similar to sea bass

Lucullus, refers to any dish that contains extremely rich &/or rare ingredients. Named after a Roman general who hosted great feasts

lyonnaise, sautéed w/mushrooms &/or onions/sauce of onions, butter & white wine ("Lyons style")

macaron, macaroon

macaroni au gratin, macaroni & cheese

macédoine, mixed fruit or mixed vegetables

macédoine de légumes, mixed vegetables

macérer, to pickle or soak

mâche, a type of lettuce

macis, the outer covering of a nutmeg/mace

Mâcon, wine from Burgundy

mâconnaise, usually refers to a goat's milk cheese

macreuse, pot roast

madeleine, butter cake

madère, w/Madeira wine

magret, breast of fattened goose or duck

maigre, lean

maïs, corn

maison, house

maître d'hôtel, head waiter/sautéed in butter w/lemon juice & parsley

maltaise, orange-flavored *hollandaise* sauce

mandarine, tangerine

mange-tout, snow pea /type of apple

mangue, mango

manière, de, in the style of

maquereau, mackerel

maraîchère, usually means w/various greens (market style)

marbré, marbled

marc, a strong liqueur made from distilling the residue of grapes (similar to Italian *grappa*). **Marc de Bandol** is a popular *marc* found in Provence

like Grappa, Marc is an acquired taste

marcassin, young wild boar *gotta try it!*

marchand de vin, red wine & shallot sauce/wine merchant

marché, market

marée, a term used to denote fresh seafood

Marengo, à la, w/eggs

marennes, flat-shelled oysters

margarine, margarine

Margaux, a red wine from Bordeaux

mariné, marinated

marinière, "sailor's style" usually means w/seafood (most often mussels) simmered in herbs & white wine

marjolaine, marjoram. This can also refer to a layered chocolate & nut cake

marmelade, marmalade

marmite, food cooked in a small casserole

marquise, mousse cake *We love Marquise!*

maroilles, strong, hard cheese

marron, chestnut

marrons au sirop, chestnuts in vanilla-flavored syrup

marrons chauds, roasted chestnuts. Served on the streets of Paris

marrons entiers au naturel, chestnuts in water (used as a stuffing, in sauces or as a vegetable)

marrons glacés, candied chestnuts *marrons glacés... I don't think so.*

marrons Mont Blanc, chestnut purée & cream on a spongecake soaked in rum

massepain, marzipan

matafan, simple cake (flour, butter, milk & eggs) made in a skillet

matelote, freshwater fish stew/fish stew (usually eel) w/wine from the French West Indies. *Matelote de veau* is veal stew w/red wine

mauresque, a drink of *pastis* w/almond & orange syrup

mauviette, meadow lark

mayonnaise, mayonnaise

médaillon, small, round cut of meat

Médoc, red wine from Bordeaux
mélange, mixture/blend
mélasses, molasses
méli-mélo, assorted seafood
méli-mélo de légumes, mixed vegetables
melon, cantaloupe
melon à l'italienne, melon w/*prosciutto*
melon d'eau, watermelon
melon de Cavaillon, similar to a canteloupe
ménagère, a basic preparation usually w/carrots, potatoes &/or
    onions (means "in the style of a housewife")
mendiants, dessert made of dry figs, raisins, almonds & nuts
menthe, mint
menthe poivrée, peppermint
menu, menu (often a fixed-price meal)
menu dégustation, set-price gourmet
    menu of specialties of the chef
menu du jour, menu of the day
menu fixe, fixed price menu
menu gastronomique, gourmet menu
menu pour enfant, children's menu
mer, sea
merda, *gnocchi* made w/Swiss chard
merenda, morning snack
merguez, spicy sausage (usually lamb)
meringues, baked shells of sweetened, beaten egg whites
merlan, whiting
merle, blackbird
Merlot, dry, medium- to
    full-bodied red wine
merlu, a type of hake
merluche, dried cod
mérou, grouper
merveille, sugar doughnut
mesclun, lettuce salad of mixed greens
messine, an herb & cream sauce

Méli-Mélo... never had it but love the name.

Mendiant means beggar.

Merguez... Our friend Samy's favorite.

Merle. I'm not sure what I'd expect if this were on a menu.

méthode champenoise, sparkling wine (natural method)

mets, dish/preparation

mets selon la saison, seasonal preparation

meunière, w/parsley butter/seasoned fish floured & fried in butter, lemon & parsley. The word means "miller's wife" which refers to the flour that is used to prepare this dish

meurette, w/red wine sauce

Meursault, wine from Burgundy

miel, honey

miettes, flakes/crumbs

mignardises, *petits fours*

mignon, tenderloin cut

mignonnette, small piece of fillet/coarsely ground white pepper

mijoté, simmered

milieu de poitrine, brisket

millas, corn-meal mush

mille feuille, light pastry w/cream filling (napoleon)

millésime, vintage

mimolette, a mild cheese

mimosa, w/chopped egg yolks

mirabeau, w/anchovies & olives

mirabelle, yellow plum/plum brandy

mireilie, à la, there are many versions of this cold marinade

mirepoix, vegetables cut into cubes

miroir pommes, apple-Bavarian cream dessert

miroton, slices. Can also refer to a meat & onion stew or a brown sauce including onions

mitonnée, a souplike dish

mixte, mixed

mode, à la, in the style of

moelle, bone/marrow

moelleux, full-bodied. This can also mean tender

moka, coffee

mollusques, shellfish

momie, thimble-sized *pastis*

[handwritten note:] Mignon means cute.

[handwritten note:] Mille feuille ~ MEEL FOY means a thousand leaves.

69

montagne, de, from the mountains

Mont Blanc, chestnut meringue topped w/a "mountain" of
    whipped cream (named after the mountain peak)

montmorency, w/cherries

morceau, piece

morille, morel mushroom (a rare,
    wild mushroom w/a smoky flavor)

mornay, white sauce w/cheese

mortadelle, bologna sausage
    w/pistachios & pickles

morue, cod

morue en rayte, cod in red wine sauce

moscovite, a dessert made in a mold w/any number of
    ingredients/a way of preparing duck

mouclade, creamy mussel soup

moule, mussel

moule de bouchot, small cultivated mussel

moule d'Espagne, large sharp-shelled mussel (frequently
    served raw)

moule de Parques, Dutch cultivated mussel

moules à la poulette, mussels in a rich white wine sauce

moules marinières, mussels simmered in white wine w/shallots

mourtayrol, chicken dish flavored w/saffron

moussaka, a Greek dish frequently found on menus in Paris. It
    is an eggplant, lamb & tomato casserole

mousse, a light & airy dish of whipped cream or beaten egg
    whites/chopped meat or fish w/eggs & cream

mousse au chocolat, chocolate mousse

mousse de foie gras, *foie gras* must have, under French law,
    fattened liver w/up to 20% other foods. *Mousse de foie*
    gras contains up to 45% other foods such as eggs, pork
    liver &/or truffles

mousseline, w/whipped cream/*hollandaise* sauce w/cream

mousseron, small wild mushroom

mousseux, sparkling

moutarde, mustard

mouton, mutton

muge, mullet (in Provence)

mulet, mullet

munster, soft, flavorful cheese (often flavored w/caraway, cumin or anise)

mûre, blackberry

muscade, nutmeg

Muscadet, a dry, white wine

muscat, dessert wine

museau, muzzle

museau de veau, calf's muzzle

myrtille, blueberry

myrtille ~ mer-tee

mystère, cooked meringue dessert w/ice cream

nage, "swimming;" served in an aromatic poaching liquid

nantua, crayfish or shrimp sauce

napolitaine, vanilla, strawberry & chocolate ice cream

nappe, tablecloth

nappé, covered in a sauce

nature, plain

naturel, plain. *Au naturel* means plainly cooked

navarin, mutton stew w/turnips

navet, turnip

nefle, small orange-colored fruit

Non, merci.

nègre, flourless chocolate cake

neige, w/beaten egg whites (means "snow")

neufchâtel, rich, creamy cheese (a lower-fat cheese)

Newburg, lobster cooked in a sauce made of butter, cream, wine (or brandy) & egg yolks. Newburg is an alteration of Wenburg, the name of the patron for whom the sauce was named

niçoise, usually means w/tomatoes, anchovies, vinegar & black olives

nid d'abeilles, honey cake

nivernaise , à la, a dish w/carrots & onions

Noilly Prat, French vermouth

noir, black

abeilles means bees.

noisette, hazelnut/round piece of meat

noix, nut/walnut. This can also refer to nuggets

noix d'acajou, cashew

noix de coco, coconut

noix de muscade, nutmeg

noix de pecan, pecan

noix de veau, top side of the leg of veal

non, not

nonats, tiny Mediterranean fish served deep fried

normande, usually means cooked w/fish, cream & mushrooms ("Normandy style"). This can also refer to a dish in a cream sauce often w/*calvados*

nougats, roasted almonds, egg whites, nuts & honey dessert

nouilles, noodles

nouilles fraîches maison, homemade fresh pasta

nouveau, new

nouveauté, new offering

nouvelle, new

noyau, pit (as in an olive pit)

Nuits-Saint-Georges, red wine from Burgundy

oeuf, egg. *Blancs d'oeufs* are egg whites & *jaunes d'oeufs* are egg yolks

oeuf à la coque, soft-boiled egg

oeuf à l'américaine, fried egg

oeuf à la russe, hard-boiled egg served cold w/diced vegetables in a mayonnaise sauce

oeuf à l'Huguenote, poached egg w/meat sauce

oeuf au plat, fried egg

oeuf brouillé, scrambled egg

(handwritten: ouef au plat~ / OOF oh PLah)

oeuf chemise, poached egg

oeuf Côte d'Azur, poached egg in an artichoke bottom

oeuf dur, hard-boiled egg

oeuf dur soubise, hard-boiled egg w/onion & cream sauce

oeuf en gelée, poached egg served in gelatin

oeuf en meurette, poached egg in a red wine sauce

oeuf farci, stuffed egg

oeuf frit, fried egg

oeuf mayonnaise, eggs & mayonnaise

oeuf mollet, soft-boiled egg

oeuf poché, poached egg

oeuf poché à la Chartres, poached egg w/tarragon

oeuf Rossini, egg w/truffles & Madeira wine. This can also be a poached egg w/*pâté*

oeufs à la diable, devilled eggs

oeufs à la neige, whipped, sweetened egg whites served in a vanilla custard sauce (means "eggs in the snow")

oeufs au lait, egg custard

oeuf sauté à la poêle, fried egg

oeufs au vin, eggs poached in red wine

oeufs d'alose, cooked fish (shad) eggs

oeufs en meurette, poached eggs w/red wine sauce from Bourgogne

oeufs pochés suzettes, poached eggs in baked potatoes

oeuf sur la plat, fried egg

offert, free ("offered")

oie, goose

oie ~
oY

oie à l'instar de visé, goose boiled & then fried. A Belgian specialty

oignon, onion

oignon sounds like agneau...

oignons grelots, small pickled onions

oiseau, bird

olives, olives

olives farcies, stuffed olives

Lamb. We've had problems here.

olives noires, black olives

olives vertes, green olives

omble-chevalier, freshwater fish of the trout family (char)

omelette, omelet

omelette au fromage, cheese omelet

omelette au jambon, ham omelet

omelette au lard, bacon omelet

omelette au naturel, plain omelet

omelette aux champignons, mushroom omelet

omelette aux fines herbs, omelet w/herbs

omelette brayaude, potato omelet

omelette César, omelet w/garlic & herbs

omelette complète, omelet w/ham & cheese

omelette fourée aux pommes dite à la Normandie, apple upside-down cake

omelette landaise, omelet w/pine nuts

omelette nature, plain omelet

omelette norvégienne, baked Alaska

omelette parmentier, potato omelet

omelette paysanne, omelet w/bacon & potatoes

omelette quercynoise, cheese & walnut omelet

onglet, flank steak

opéra, layered spongecake w/chocolate sauce

orange, orange

orange givrée, orange sorbet served in an orange

orange pressée, fresh, squeezed orange juice

oranges en rondelles, candied orange slices in orange jelly

oreilles, ears

oreillettes, pastry puffs

orge, barley

orgeat, almond-sugar syrup

origon, oregano

orties, nettles

ortolan, small game bird

os, bone

os à moelle, marrow bone

oseille, sorrel

ostendaise, w/shrimp & oysters

ou, or

ouassous, large crayfish found in the French West Indies

oursin, sea urchin

pacanes, pecans (in Guadeloupe)

päella, saffron-flavored rice & various ingredients. There are many variations of this famous Spanish dish found on many menus in France

pagre commun, sea bream
paillard, thin, flattened piece of meat, poultry or fish fillet
pailles pommes, fried, shredded potatoes
paillettes, cheese straws
pain, bread
pain au chocolat, chocolate-filled pastry
pain au lait, sweet bun
pain aux noix, walnut bread
pain aux raisins, bun w/custard & white raisins
pain blanc, white bread
pain complet, whole-wheat bread
pain de campagne, chewy "country" bread
pain de mie, sliced white bread (sandwich bread)
pain d'épices, gingerbread/a dense spice cake w/honey
pain de seigle, rye bread
pain de son, bran bread
pain de sucre, sugar loaf
pain grillé, toast
pain noir, dark bread
pain ordinaire, French bread
pain perdu, French toast
pain viennois, Vienna loaf
palaia, small sardines & anchovies
palais, cookies. *Palais de dames* are fruit cookies
paleron, shoulder of beef
paletot, skin, bone & meat of a fattened goose or duck (after the liver is removed)
palets de marrons, puréed-chestnut patties
palette de porc, pork shoulder
palmier, palm hearts (*coeurs de palmier*)
palmiers, caramelized puff pastry
paloise, *béarnaise* sauce w/mint
palombe, pigeon
palourdes, clams
pamplemousse, grapefruit ←
panaché, mixed

paillard ~
pie-yard

Pain... pronounced pan with the slightest hint of an "N"

Isn't this a great word?

75

panade, thick mixture used to bind dumplings (panada)

panais, parsnip

pan bagnat, large round sandwich filled w/olive oil, onions, olives, tomatoes, anchovies & a hard-boiled egg. A specialty on the Côte d'Azur (means "wet bread"). This is a *salade niçoise* sandwich

pané, breaded

panier, basket

panisses, chickpea-flour pancake (deep fried)

panne de porc, fat from the kidneys of a pig

pannequet, rolled, filled crêpe

papalines, orange-flavored chocolates from Avignon

papeton d'aubergines, eggplant casserole from Avignon (means "eggplant of the popes")

papillons, butterfly cookies

papillote, en, baked in parchment paper

paquets, en, in packages or parcels

parfait, ice-cream dessert. Can also refer to goose, duck or chicken-liver mousse

parfum, flavor

Paris-Brest, ring-shaped *éclair* filled w/praline cream

parisienne, a vegetable garnish w/potatoes sautéed in butter w/a white sauce

parme, amberjack (in Provence)

parmentier, dish containing potatoes

part, portion

partager, to share

passe-pierre, seaweed

Passe-Tout-Grain, red wine from Burgundy

pasta, pasta. Originally from neighboring Italy, pasta is an important part of provençal cuisine

pastèque, watermelon

pastèque

pastilles, hard, fruit-flavored candy

pastis, anise-flavored aperitif. This is a provençal word meaning mixture. It is a summer drink. Common brands are Pastis 51, Pernod, Ricard, Granier, Prado & Henri Bardouin

pastis landais, a sweet bread dessert

patate, sweet potato

patate douce, sweet potato

pâte, pastry dough.
  This can also mean a batter or paste.
  Do not confuse this w/*pâté*

pâte à choux, cream-puff pastry

pâte à foncer, shortbread crust

pâte à frire, sweet french-frying batter

pâte à pain, bread dough

pâte brisée, pie pastry

pâte d'amandes, marzipan

pâte de fruits, fruit-paste candies

pâte feuilletée, puff pastry

pâte levée, bread dough

pâte sablée, sweet pie pastry

pâte sucrée, sweet pie pastry

pâté, pâté

pâté ardennais, purée of pork in a loaf of bread

pâté de campagne, *pâté* w/a variety of meats

pâté de canard, duck *pâté*

pâté de foie de volaille, chicken-liver *pâté*

pâté de foie d'oie, *pâté* that contains at least 50% goose liver &
  up to 50% other meats

pâté de foie gras, goose-liver *pâté*. Contains at least 75% goose
  liver

pâté doré, seasoned baked pork-liver *pâté* served cold

pâté en croûte, *pâté* in a pastry crust

pâté en pot, mutton soup found in the French West Indies

pâté maison et rillettes, a slice of a loaf of ground seasoned
  meat

pâtes, pasta

pâtisserie, pastry

patte, foot (paw) or leg of an animal or bird

patte blanche, small crayfish

patte rouge, large crayfish

Mind your diacritical marks!

Pâte is generally pastry.

Pâté is a meat purée

Pâtes is pasta

Pauillac, rich red wine from Bordeaux

Pauillac
Poo-yak

paupiette, slice of veal rolled around stuffing

pavé, thick slice of beef (or calf's liver)

pavé aux marrons, chestnut & chocolate cake

pavot, graines de, poppy seeds

paysanne, à la, "country style" usually means a
dish containing assorted vegetables

pays d'auge, cream & cider sauce

pays, du, from the area

peau, skin

pêche, peach

pêche.

pêche melba, peaches w/ice cream & raspberry sauce

pêcheur, this term refers to fish preparations (means
"fisherman")

pelardons, goat cheese

pelé, peeled

pelure, peelings

perce-pierre, seaweed

perdrix.

perche, perch

perdreau, young partridge

perdrix, partridge

périgourdine, à la, w/goose- or duck-liver purée & truffles

périgueux, a brown sauce w/chopped truffles

Pernod, anise-flavored aperitif

perroquet, a drink of *pastis* & mint

petit beure
little butter

persil, parsley. *Persillé* means parslied

persillade, chopped parsley & garlic

pesto, see *pistou*

pétillant, slightly sparkling beverage

petit, small

petit four ~
little oven

petit beurre, tea biscuit

petit déjeuner, breakfast

petite friture, whitebait

petit four, small fancy cookie or cake

petit gâteau, small cake

petit-gris, small snail

petit noir, black coffee
petit pain, roll. *Petits pains au maïs* are made w/corn meal
petit pois, pea
petit pois de cérons, peas w/pork
petit salé, salt pork
petits farcis provençaux, stuffed vegetables of Provence
petits gâteaux, cookies
petits pois, peas

Bien sur!

petits pois à la Normandie, creamed peas
petit-suisse, creamy, unsalted cheese from Normandy /cheese
    beignets
pétoncle, tiny scallop
pets de nonne, small fried pastry
pibale, small eel
pichet, pitcher of wine
picodon, goat's-milk cheese from Provence
picon bière, beer mixed w/a sweet liqueur
pièce, piece/each
pied, foot
pied de cochon, pig's foot
pied de mouton, wild mushroom/sheep's foot
pied de porc, pig's foot
pieps et paquets, stuffed-tripe dish   *No thanks*
pietra, chestnut-flavored beer from Corsica
pieuvre, oysters
pigeon, pigeon
pigeonneau, young pigeon
pignatelle, small cheese fritter
pignons, pine nuts/croissant w/pine nuts
pilaf/pilau, rice cooked w/broth & onions
piment, chili pepper/pimento
piment doux, sweet pepper
piment en poudre, chili powder
piment poivre de Jamaïque, allspice
pimprenelle, burnet (a green used in salads)
pince, claw

pineau, cognac & grape juice

pintade, guinea hen

pintadeau, young guinea hen

pipérade, omelet w/ham, green peppers, tomatoes & garlic

piquant, spicy hot

piquante, sauce of pickles or capers, shallots & vinegar

piqué, larded

pissala, fish purée used in *pissaladière*

pissaladière, pizza-like tart w/onions,
      black olives & purée of anchovies
      & sardines (from Provence)

pissenlit, dandelion leaves

pistache, pistachio

pistil de safran, thread of saffron

pissenlit.

pistou, garlic, basil, nuts & olive-oil sauce (known as pesto in
      Italy)/pesto soup

pithiviers, puff pastry filled w/ground almonds & sweet cream

pizza, pizza is not shared in France, is not eaten w/your
      hands & will be served w/a bottle of olive oil w/hot
      peppers at the bottom. The oil is to spice up your pizza.
      A cheese & tomato pizza is called a ***marguerite***

pizza quatres saisons, four-seasons pizza (four toppings: ham,
      mushrooms, cheese & anchovy)

pizza reine, pizza topped w/ham & mushrooms

planteurs, rum & fruit punches found in the French West Indies

plaque de chocolat, chocolate bar

plat, plate/dish

plat de résistance, main course

plat du jour, plate (special) of the day

plate, flat-shelled oyster. This can also
      refer to water w/out carbonation

Le Plat is usually the main course

plateau, platter

plateau de fromages, platter of cheeses. In Normandy, this is
      almost always served w/*calvados*

plat froid, cold plate

plat principal (plats principaux), main course(s)

pleurote, grey mushroom found in Loire
plie, flounder/plaice
plie franche, flounder
plombières, vanilla ice-cream dessert
    w/whipped cream & candied fruit
pluviers, plovers (small birds)
poché, poached
pochouse, fish & onion stew
    prepared w/wine (from Bourgogne)
poêle, à la, fried
point, à, medium done. In France, this means still pink
pointe, tip. *Pointe d'asperge* is an asparagus tip
poire, pear
poireau (poireaux), leek(s)
poire Belle Hélène, pear w/ice cream & chocolate sauce
poirier d'anjou, pear cake
pois, peas
pois chiche, chick-pea
pois mange-tout, snow pea
poisson, fish
poisson à grande friture, deep-dried fish
poisson d'eau douce, freshwater fish
poisson de mer, saltwater fish
poissonnerie, fish soup/fish store
poitrine, breast
poitrine d'agneau Sainte Ménéhould, braised & grilled lamb
    breast
poitrine demi-sel, slab of unsmoked bacon
poitrine de mouton, mutton breast
poitrine de porc, pork belly
poitrine de veau, veal breast
poitrine fumée, slab of smoked bacon
poivrade, brown sauce of wine, vegetables, peppers & vinegar
poivre, pepper. *Au poivre* means w/peppercorns
poivre d'Ain, flavored *banon*
poivre d'ane, bitter, peppery herb

[handwritten note:] Poêle means stove or frying pan.

[handwritten label:] poire.

poivre de cayenne, very hot red pepper

poivre de Chine, mouth-numbing type of peppercorn

poivre de la Jamaïque, allspice (the main ingredient of jerk seasoning)

poivre frais de Madagascar, green peppercorns

poivre mignonette, crushed peppercorns used on steaks

poivre noir, black peppercorns

poivre rose, pink peppercorns

poivre vert, green peppercorns

poivron, bell pepper

poivron doux, sweet bell pepper

poivron épicé, hot pepper

poivron rouge, red pepper

poivron vert, green pepper

polenta, corn meal/polenta (dish of cooked corn meal, water w/butter & cheese)

Pomerol, a red wine (merlot) from Bordeaux

pommade, a thick paste

pomme, apple

pomme au four, potato baked in its skin

pomme bonne femme, baked apple

pomme de terre, potato

pomme de terre brayaude, oven-cooked potato

pomme en l'air, caramelized apple slices served w/blood sausage

pommes à l'anglaise, boiled potatoes

pommes allumettes, very thin french fries

pommes anna, sliced & layered potato & onion dish

pommes boulangère, a potato & meat dish/sliced potatoes w/onions

pommes château, potatoes sautéed in butter

pommes dauphine, potatoes mashed in butter & egg yolks, mixed in flour & deep fried

pommes dauphinoise, potatoes baked w/garlic, cheese & milk

pommes de terre à la berrichonne, herbed potatoes

pommes de terre à l'angoumois, potato & cabbage casserole

poivron.

pomme.

pommes de terre... potatoes are often called pommes... apples.

pommes duchesse, potatoes mashed in butter & egg yolks
pommes en robe de chambre, potatoes in their skin
pommes en robe des champs, potatoes in their skin
pommes fondantes, potatoes cooked in butter
pommes frites, french fries
pommes gratinées, potatoes baked w/cheese
pommes lyonnaises, potatoes sautéed w/onions
pommes mousseline, mashed potatoes
pommes nature, boiled or steamed potatoes
pommes nouvelles, new potatoes
pommes paille, fried strips of potatoes
pommes Pont-Neuf, french fries
pommes renversées, baked caramelized apple pudding
pommes sautées, fried potatoes
pommes soufflées, puffy slices of potatoes fried twice
pommes vapeur, steamed or boiled potatoes
pompe à l'huile, sweet flat bread flavored w/olive oil
pont l'évêque, strong, flavored, semi-hard cheese (usually served in square blocks)
porc, pork
porc au lait, pork cooked in milk
porc aux deux pommes, pork w/potatoes & apples
porc demi-sel, salted pork
porcelet, young suckling pig
porchetta/porketta, this can refer to the Italian dish of roast suckling pig stuffed w/herbs. Around Nice, this can be an enormous tube of pig skin (with the pig's head attached) stuffed with organ meats and unidentifiable items and served in round slices as large as your plate.
porc salé, salted pork
Porto, port
porto, au, w/port
port-salut/port du salut, mild, soft, buttery cheese
portugaises, a type of oyster
potable, drinkable

pont l'évèque means Bishop's Bridge.

potage, soup (usually thick)

potage à la crème de coco, cream-of-coconut soup found in the French West Indies

potage au cerfeuil, soup of chervil & other herbs. A specialty in the Ardennes region of Belgium

potage bilbi, fish & oyster soup

potage bonne femme, potato & leek soup ← *Love this*

potage cancalais, fish soup

potage Crécy, carrot soup

potage crème normande, cream of fish soup

potage cressonière, watercress soup

potage cultivateur, soup w/mixed vegetables & pork

potage d'Auvergne, lentil & potato soup

potage de Père Tranquille, lettuce soup

potage du Barry, cauliflower soup

potage Longchamp, soup featuring peas

potage nivernaise, carrot soup

potage parmentier, leek & potato soup

potage portugais, tomato *potage*

potage printanier, vegetable soup

potage Saint-Germain, split-pea soup

potage soissonnais, haricot-bean soup

potage velouté, creamy soup

pot-au-feu, stew of meat & vegetables

pot-de-crème, mousse or custard dessert. In Provence, it's usually lemon custard

potée, boiled pork (or beef) w/cabbage

pothine de boeuf, beef braised w/*calvados*. The *pothine* is a cast-iron casserole in which this dish is cooked

potiron, pumpkin

Pouilly-Fuissé, dry white wine from Burgundy

poularde, capon/fatted chicken

poularde Saint-Hélène, chicken w/dumplings

poule, hen

poule au pot, stewed chicken w/vegetables

poule au riz, hen served w/rice

poule d'Inde, turkey hen

poule faisane, pheasant

poule farcie en daube à la berrichonne, boned, stuffed chicken in jelly. A specialty in Central France

poulet, chicken

poulet basquaise, chicken w/sweet peppers & tomatoes ("Basque style")

poulet Biarritz, chicken in white wine

poulet chasseur, chicken usually w/mushrooms & white wine. This can also be chicken served w/tomato sauce

poulet créole, chicken in a white sauce (often spicy) & served w/rice

poulet de Bresse, free-range, corn-fed chicken

poulet de grain, corn-fed chicken

poulet de Saint-Astier, chicken stew

poulet fermier, free-range chicken

poulet Marengo, chicken cooked in white wine w/tomatoes, garlic, mushrooms & shallots. Said to be the chicken dish served to Napoleon after the battle of Marengo in 1800

poulet rôti, roast chicken

pourboire means for to drink

poulpe, octopus

pourboire, tip

pour emporter, to go/take out

pourpier, purslane (a green used in salads)

pousse-pierre, seaweed

poussin, spring chicken

praire, clam

praline, caramelized almonds

premier cru, denotes a high quality wine

pré-salé, lambs that graze on salt meadows

pressé, fresh squeezed

presse, à la, pressed

pression, draft beer.
   À la pression means from the tap

pression.

primeur, early season or spring fruits & vegetables

Prince-de-Galle, stuffed w/*pâté*

85

printanière, à la, w/spring vegetables

prisuttu, cured ham from Corsica

prix, price

prix fixe, fixed price

prix net, service is included

Profiteroles our favorite French dessert!

profiterole, cream puff filled w/ice cream & covered in chocolate sauce

provençale, à la, w/garlic, onions, herbs & tomatoes ("Provence style"). Provence is one of France's wine-grow ing regions &, of course, one of the world's best-known & loved tourist destinations

prune, plum

pruneau/pruneau sec, prune

pudding, custard/pudding

puits d'amour, pastry filled w/custard

Puits d'amour means Well of love.

pulenta, chestnut-flour bread from Corsica

purée, strained fruit or vegetables. *En purée* means mashed

purée de pommes de terre, mashed potatoes

pyramide au chocolat, chocolate pyramid filled w/chocolate pieces & sauces, whipped cream & butter

quartiers d'orange glacés, caramelized orange sections. A dessert found on menus in Provence

quart, un, on a menu this denotes a quarter-liter of wine

quatre-épices, a blend of four spices (nutmeg, cloves, ginger & white pepper)

quatre-quarts, Madeira cake

quenelle, dumpling

quenelles de foie de veau, calf's-liver dumplings. A specialty in Luxembourg

quetsche, small plum/liquor made from plums

queue, tail

queue de boeuf, oxtail

quiche, egg tart w/vegetable or meat filling

quiche au fromage blanc, bacon & white cheese *quiche*

quiche lorraine, *quiche* w/cheese, bacon & onions

râble, loin of rabbit

râble de lièvre, saddle of rabbit

racasse, scorpion fish

raclette, cheese heated until it begins to melt. The melted part is scraped off & placed on a warm plate to be eaten w/boiled potatoes, pickles & pickled onions. This can also refer to melted cheese on a *baguette*

radis, radish

radis noir, large black radish

ragoût, stewed/meat stew

raie, ray/skate (fish)

raifort, horseradish

raisin, grape

raisins de Corinthe, currants

raisins de table, dessert grapes

raisin sec, raisin

Raisins.

raïto, red wine, tomato & onion sauce

ramequin, small cheese tart or a small casserole

rancio, dessert wine

râpé, shredded/grated. *La râpée* is a creamed-potato pancake

rascasse, fish found in the Mediterranean (scorpion fish)

ratatouille, eggplant casserole

rave, root vegetable

ravigote, vinegar dressing (w/herbs & shallots)

ravioli, ravioli. Common in Nice & all of the French Riviera

reblochon, soft, strong cheese

refroidi, chilled

*à la reine...
like the
Queen.*

régional(e), from the region/local

reine, à la, w/mince meat or poultry

reine-claude, small green or yellow plums (greengage)

reinette, fall & winter apple

religieuse, *éclair* cake

rémoulade, mayonnaise sauce

renversée, turned out of its cooking container

repas, meal

Rhône, this valley is one of France's wine regions (located in South Central France) & known for its white wines

rhubarbe, rhubarb

rhum, rum

Ricard, anise-flavored aperitif

Richelieu, à la, w/tomatoes, bacon & potatoes

rigotte, goat cheese

rillettes, highly seasoned pork, duck or goose baked in its own fat (potted meat)

rillons, pork belly

ris, sweetbreads

ris d'agneau, lamb sweetbreads

ris de..., sweetbreads

ris de veau, veal sweetbreads (the pancreas of a veal calf)

You won't want to confuse ris and riz...

rissole, pastry/meat or fish patty

rissolé, fried until brown & crisp

riz, rice. *Crème de riz* is rice flour (very finely gound rice)

riz à l'impératrice, rice pudding

riz basquais, spicy rice

riz complet, brown rice

rizotto, risotto

riz pilaf, rice boiled in bouillon w/onions (rice pilaf)

riz safrané, saffron rice

riz sauvage, wild rice

robe des champs, en, in its skin

Robert, a brown sauce w/onions, white wine & mustard

rocambole, a member of the onion family

rognon, kidney

rognonnade, veal loin

rognons blancs, testicles

rognons de veau à la liégeoise, roast veal kidneys. A specialty in Belgium

romarin, rosemary

romsteck, rump steak

rondelle, round slice

roquefort, blue cheese ← *Do you mean to tell me you had to look this up?*

roquette, arugula (rocket)

rosbif, roast beef

rosé, rosé. This can also refer to rare meat

rosette, dried sausage/small round piece

Rossini, a dish that includes *foie gras* & truffles

rôti, roast/roasted

rouelle, a slice cut at an angle

rouelle de veau, veal shank

rouge, red

rouget, red mullet

rouille, spicy sauce of peppers, garlic & tomatoes

rouilleuse, red garlic mayonnaise

roulade, rolled slice of meat or fish w/stuffing/"Swiss roll"
    dessert w/cream or jam stuffing

roulé, rolled

rouleau, roll of...

roussillonnade, grilled sausage & mushroom dish

roux, flour & butter mixture (used to thicken sauces or soup)

rouzoles, crêpes filled w/bacon & ham

rumsteck, rump steak

sabayon, creamy dessert of wine, sugar, egg yolks &
    flavoring/cream wine sauce

sablé, shortbread cookie

saccharine, saccharin

sachet de thé, tea bag

safran, saffron

Saint Amour ...
Holy Love.

saignant, very rare

saindoux, pork fat

Saint-Amour, red wine from Beaujolais

Saint-Emilion, red wine form Bordeaux

Saint-Estèphe, red wine from Bordeaux

Saint-Germain, w/peas

Saint-Honore, cake w/cream

Saint-Hubert, sauce w/bacon & chestnuts

Saint-Jacques, sea scallop

Saint-Julien, red wine from Bordeaux

Saint-Marcellin, goats' cheese w/a smoky flavor

Saint-Raphaël, quinine flavored aperitif

Saint-Paulin, mild, semi-soft cheese
Saint-Pierre John Dory fish (a mackerel)
saison, season
salade, salad
salade antiboise, salad usually w/fish, capers & green peppers
salade au bleu, salad w/blue cheese (& frequently walnuts)
salade au chapon, salad served on toast rubbed w/garlic
salade aux noix, green salad w/walnuts
salade cauchoise, ham, potato & celery salad
salade chiffonnade, shredded lettuce & sorrel
salade composée, chef's salad
salade d'Auvergne, salad w/blue cheese dressing
salade de boulghour, bulgur-wheat salad
salade de crudités, chopped-vegetable salad
salade de fruits, fruit cocktail
salade de gésiers, green salad w/gizzards *Non, merci.*
salade de liège, bean & potato salad. A specialty in Belgium
salade de museau de boeuf, marinated beef headcheese
salade de saison, seasonal salad
salade de tomates, tomato salad
salade folle, mixed salad usually w/green beans
salade lyonnaise, *hors d'oeuvre* of seasoned meats in an oil,
      shallot & vinegar dressing
salade mélangée, mixed salad
salade mêlée, mixed salad
salade mesclun, mixed greens
salade mixte, mixed salad
salade multicolore, salad w/radishes, peppers, egg, cucumber,
      corn & basil
salade niçoise, salad usually w/tomatoes, anchovies or tuna,
      potatoes, vinegar & black olives (served as a main course)
salade panachée, mixed salad
salade paysanne, salad w/eggs & pieces of bacon
salade russe, diced vegetables in mayonnaise
salade simple, green salad
salade verte, green salad

salade wallonie, warm salad w/lettuce, bacon & fried potatoes. A specialty in Belgium

The Walloons are the French speaking Belgians.

salaisons, an hors d'oeuvre of olives, anchovies &/or herring

salé, salted

salicorne, algae used as a condiment

salmis, roasted game or poultry

salpicon, stuffing w/sauce

salsifis, salsify (oyster plant)

Sancerre, white & pale, light-bodied red wines from the Loire Valley

sandre, pike

sandwich, sandwich

sandwich au fromage, cheese sandwich

sandwich au jambon, ham sandwich

sandwich au saucisson, sausage sandwich

sandwich aux rillettes, *pâté* sandwich

sandwich crudités, lettuce &/or chopped vegetable sandwich

sang, blood

sanglier, wild boar

sans, without

sans arêtes, boneless

sans peau, skinless

sarcelle, teal (river duck)

sardine, sardine

Sardines.

sarrasin, buckwheat

sarriette, summer savory (an herb)

sartando, small fried fish w/hot vinegar

sartenais, hard, strong cheese from Corsica

sauce, sauce/gravy/salad dressing

sauce à la crème, cream sauce

sauce aurore, a white sauce w/tomato purée

sauce aux câpres, a white sauce w/capers

sauce bigarade, orange sauce

sauce bretonne, egg, butter & mustard sauce

sauce café de Paris, cream, mustard & herb sauce
sauce catalane, tomato, orange & garlic sauce
sauce gaillarde, seasoned mayonnaise
sauce mornay, cheese sauce
sauce poulette, mushroom, egg yolk & wine sauce
sauce soubise, onion sauce
sauce Suzette, orange sauce
sauce velouté, creamy soup/white sauce (*roux* mixed w/poultry, fish, veal or mushroom stock)
sauce vinot, wine sauce
saucisse, sausage
saucisse à l'ail tiède, garlic sausage (served warm)
saucisse à la navarraise, sausage w/wine & sweet peppers
saucisse de Francfort, hot dog/frankfurter *Saucisson is*
saucisse de Strasbourg, beef sausage *dried sausage*
saucisse de Toulouse, fresh pork sausage *like Salami.*
saucisson, dried sausage
saucisson à l'alsacienne, poached sausage w/horseradish sauce
saucisson à la lyonnaise, poached sausage w/potato salad
saucisson chaud de Lyon en croûte, red sausage w/cubes of fat & baked in pastry
saucisson de Lyon, dried seasoned sausage
sauge, sage *Sauge.*
saumon, salmon
saumon de l'Atlantique, Atlantic salmon
saumon fumé, smoked salmon
Saumur-Champigny, light-bodied red wine from the Loire Valley
saupiquet, spicy cream sauce w/bread crumbs
saupiquet des amognes, ham w/spicy cream sauce
sauté, sautéed
Sauternes, a fruity white wine
sauvage, wild
Sauvignon de Touraine, white wine from the *Sauvignon Blanc* grape
savarin, spongecake topped w/rum & cream

Savoie, one of France's wine-growing regions

savoyarde, flavored w/cheese. *À la savoyarde* also can refer to
    a vermouth & cream sauce

scampi, prawns

scarole, escarole, a salad green (a type of *endive*)

scotch, scotch

sec, dry/straight

séché, dried

seiche, large squid/cuttlefish

seiches farcies, cuttlefish stuffed w/a mixture of sausage & the
    meat of cuttlefish tentacles

seigle, rye

sel, salt

sel-épicé, salt spiced w/basil, nutmeg, cloves, cinnamon,
    peppercorns, bay leaves & coriander

sel gemme, rock salt

sel gris, coarse rock or sea salt

selle, saddle of meat, generally the loin roast

selle anglaise, saddle of meat

sel marin, sea salt

selon arrivage, on a menu, this means the dish
    depends on availability

selon grandeur/salon grosseur, price paid by the size or weight

sel raffiné, refined salt

semoule, semolina flour

sériole, amber jack, a type of fish

serpolet, wild thyme

serran, perch

service compris, service included

service non compris, service not include

serviette, napkin

s.g., abbreviation for price paid by the size or weight

sherry, sherry

sirop, syrup

sirop de sucre d'érable, maple syrup

smitane, cream, wine & onion sauce

socca, wood oven-baked corn-meal bread served on the Côte
d'Azur

soissons, white beans

soja, soy

sole, sole

sole normande, sole in a butter, onion, mushroom, white wine,
cream & *calvados* sauce

son, bran

sorbet, sherbet

soubise, onion sauce

soubise-aurore, onion & tomato sauce

soucoupe, saucer

soufflé, soufflé (beaten egg whites
w/various ingredients baked in a mold)

soufflé à la reine, soufflé w/poultry or meat

soufflé au Grand Marnier, soufflé w/orange liqueur

soufflé Rothschild, vanilla-flavored fruit soufflé

soupe, soup

soupe à l'oignon gratinée, French onion soup

soupe au pistou, vegetable & noodle soup (soup w/pesto found
in the South of France)

soupe corse, Corsican soup of vegetables & herbs simmered
w/a ham bone

soupe de montagne, Corsican soup of vegetables & herbs
simmered w/a ham bone

soupe de poisson, fish soup

soupe paysanne, Corsican soup of vegetables & herbs
simmered w/a ham bone

soupe pêcheur, fish soup

spaghetti, spaghetti

spats, small fish of the herring family

spécialité, specialty

spécialité de la maison, house specialty

spécialité du chef, chef's specialty

spécialités locales, local dishes

steak, steak

Soucoupe means under cup... clever.

Spats... we have these in our own family.

steak au poivre, steak topped w/crushed peppercorns. ***Steak au poivre vert*** is steak in a green-peppercorn sauce & ***steak au poivre rouge*** is steak in a red-peppercorn sauce

steak frites, steak & french fries

steak haché, hamburger

steak tartare, raw steak (usually topped w/a raw egg)

stockfish, niçoise spicy fish stew

stufatu, Corsican stew w/pasta   *Love this!*

succès au pralin, meringue cake w/almonds

sucettes, lollipops ("suckers")

suchi, sushi

sucre, sugar

sucre candi, candy sugar

sucre de canne roux, brown sugar

sucre filé, spun sugar

suprême, chicken-based sauce/breast of chicken or game or fillet of fish w/an unusual combination of ingredients

suprême de volaille, chicken breast. Usually a boned chicken breast in a creamy sauce

sur commande, to your special order

surgelé(s), frozen food

surlonge, beef chuck roast

sus, en, in addition

Suze, an aperitif flavored w/gentian, an herb

tablier de sapeur, grilled breaded tripe

tagine/tajine, stew (lamb, veal or chicken) w/vegetables. This spicy stew is a specialty in North Africa (especially Morocco)

tanche, the freshwater fish tench

tapenade, mixture of black olives, olive oil, lemon juice, capers & anchovies (a spread from Provence)

tarama, mullet-roe spread

tartare, chopped raw beef/in a salad, this refers to a mayonnaise-based sauce

tarte, pie/tart

tarte à l'oignon, onion & cream tart

tarte alsacienne, apple & custard tart

tarte au citron meringuée, lemon meringue pie

tarte au fruit, fruit tart

tartelette, small tart

tarte tatin, upside-down apple tart. Legend has it that this tart was "created" when the Tatin sisters (who operated a restaurant) put the tart in the oven & left for church. They discovered their mistake, turned it upside down & served it anyway.

tarte tropézienne, yellow cake w/custard filling (created by a Polish baker in 1955 in St Tropez)

tartine, open-faced sandwich (half baguette w/butter)

tasse, cup

Tavel, rosé wine from the Côte du Rhône region

tendre, tender

tendre de tranche, round steak

tendron, breast

tendron de veau, veal breast

terrine, *pâté*/prepared in an earthenware dish

terrine de campagne, pork & liver *pâté*

terrine de légumes, ground & seasoned vegetable loaf

terrinée, caramel-rice pudding

tête, head

tête de veau vinaigrette, calf's head w/vinegar & oil dressing

teurgoule, caramel-rice pudding

thé, tea

thé au lait, tea w/milk

thé citron, tea w/ lemon

thé glacé, iced tea

thé nature, tea w/out milk

thon, tuna

thon mirabeau, tuna cooked in eggs & milk

thym, thyme

tian, a dish (usually rice, vegetables & cheese) cooked in an

The delicious sounding Tartine Beurée is just buttered bread.

Oh mon dieu, non!

Tasse du thé.

oval-shaped earthenware dish used on the Côte d'Azur

tian de Saint-Jacques et légumes provençal, sea scallops on a bed of chopped vegetables

tiède, lukewarm

tilleul, herb tea

timbale, cup. *En timbale* means meat, fish or fruit in a mold

ti punch, rum, lime & sugarcane syrup drink found in the French West Indies

ti punch is actually petit punch

tisane, herbal tea

toast, toast (little pieces of crispy bread)

tomate, tomato. This also is the name for a drink of *pastis* mixed w/grenadine

tomates à la provençal, baked tomatoes stuffed w/bread crumbs, garlic & parsley

tomates concassées, roughly chopped tomatoes

tomates farcies, tomatoes stuffed w/seasoned bread crumbs

tomme (or tome) au marc, the crust of this smooth & creamy cheese is made of grape pulp. Also known as *fondu aux raisins*

tomme (de Savoie), soft, mild cheese

tonique, tonic

tonneaux en chêne, oak barrels

topinambour, Jerusalem artichoke

tortue, turtle

tortue véritable, turtle soup

toulousaine, usually means served w/sweetbreads or truffles ("Toulouse style")

tourain, bread & garlic soup

tourin bordelais, French onion soup (usually w/bread on the bottom of the bowl)

tournedos, round cut of prime steak

tournedos Rossini, *tournedos* served w/Madeira wine sauce & served w/*foie gras* &/or truffles

tourta da blea, Swiss-chard pie

tourte, pie

tourteau, large crab

tourte aux blettes, sweet tart of eggs, cheese, raisins, pine nuts & chard

tourte du jour, savory pie of the day

tourtière, pastry filled w/prunes &/or apples. Also the name for a cooking dish

tourton, pastry filled w/prunes, apples, spinach & garlic

tout compris, everything is included in the price

tout épice, allspice

tranche, slice. *Tranché* means sliced

tranche grasse, sirloin tip

tranche napolitaine, slice of layered ice cream

travers de porc, spareribs

treipen, black pudding & sausages w/potatoes. A specialty of Luxembourg

très, very

trifle, trifle

tripe, tripe

tripe à la luxembourgoise, tripe specialty found in Luxembourg

tripes à la mode, tripe in butter, onions & *calvados*. A popular dish in Normandy

tripes à la mode de Caen, tripe baked w/calf's feet

tripes à la mode de narbonnaise, tripe in tomato sauce

Triple Sec, orange liqueur

tripoux, mutton tripe

trompettes des mort, wild mushrooms

tronçon, large slice of meat or fish

trouchia, trout. In Provence, this referes to an omelet

truffat, potato-cream pie

truffe, truffle. *Truffé* means w/truffles. Truffles are extremely expensive wild fungi that grow around the roots of trees

truffettes dauphinoise, chocolate truffles

truite, trout

truite à l'ardennaise, Belgian dish of trout cooked in a wine sauce

[handwritten note: Tripoux... Sounds fancy, still tripe.]

[handwritten note: Bien sur!]

[handwritten note: Truite.]

truite au bleu, poached trout
truite meunière, trout in a parsley & butter sauce
truite saumonée, salmon trout
ttoro, Basque mixed-fish dish
tuile, almond cookie *Love these!*
turbon, ingredients cooked in a ring mold
turbot, turbot, a fish
turbotin, small turbot
vacherin, mellow Swiss cheese
vacherin glacée, baked meringue dessert
valençay, goat's-milk cheese
Vallée d'Ange, w/cooked apples & cream (named after a region in Normandy)
vanille, vanilla
vanneau, small bird
vapeur, steamed
varié/variés, assorted
veau, veal
veau Marengo, veal w/garlic, tomatoes, white wine & cognac
végétarien, vegetarian
velouté, creamy soup/white sauce (*roux* mixed w/poultry, fish, veal or mushroom stock)
velouté d'asperges, creamy white-asparagus soup
venaison, venison
ventre, stomach/belly
ventrèche, salted & seasoned pork belly
vénus, clam
verdures, green salad vegetables
verjus, the juice of unripened grapes
vermicelle, pasta used in soup
vermouth, vermouth
vernis, large clam
verre, glass
vert, green/a sauce of spinach, mayonnaise & herbs

We like to eat venison whenever we can. Less deer left in the world to destroy our garden.

Verjus is sometimes used like vinegar.

99

vert-pré, watercress garnish

verveine, the herbal tea lemon verbena

vessie, cooked in a pig's bladder

viande, meat

viande séchée, thin slices of cured beef

viandes froides, cold meats

vichy, w/glazed carrots

vichyssoise, cold leek & potato soup

vieille, old

vieille cure, wine-distilled liqueur

vieille prune, plum-based *eau-de-vie*

vierge beurre, a simple butter sauce w/lemon juice, salt & pepper

vierge huile d'olive, virgin olive oil

vieux, old

vigneronne, sauce w/grapes & wine

vigne, sarments de, vine cuttings used w/grilled foods

vin, wine

vinaigre, vinegar

vinaigre balsamique, balsamic vinegar

vinaigre de vin, wine vinegar

vinaigrette, generally a salad dressing of vinegar, mustard, herbs & oil

vin blanc, white wine

vin chambré, wine served at room temperature

vin cuit, sweet dessert wine

Vin Délimité de Qualité Supérieure (VDQS), denotes a local wine made according to strict standards

vin de maison, house wine

vin de paille, straw wine w/a strong flavor & aroma

vin de pays, wine guaranteed to originate in a certain region ("country wine")

vin de table, table wine

vin de xérès, sherry

vin doux, sweet wine/dessert wine

vin doux naturel, naturally sweet wine

[handwritten marginal notes:]
Vielle ~ / yee-ay
Vieux ~ / vee-uh

100

vin du pays, local wine
vin gris, pink wine
vin jaune, yellow wine
vin liquoreaux, sweet wine
vin mousseux, sparkling wine
vin nouveau, new wine
vin ordinaire, table wine
vin rosé, rosé wine
vin rouge, red wine
vin sec, dry wine
violet de Provence, braid of garlic
violette, crystallized violet petals
vivant/vivante, alive/living
vodka, vodka
volaille, poultry
vol-au-vent, puff pastry filled w/fish, meat &/or sweetbreads
waterzooi, chicken or fish poached in a sauce w/vegetables. A
     Belgian specialty
waterzooi de poulet, chicken poached in a sauce w/vegetables
whisky, whisky
Williamine, a pear brandy
xérès, sherry
yaourt/yogourt, yogurt
Yvorne, a dry Swiss white wine
zeste, citrus zest
zeste de citron, lemon zest
zeste de citron confits, candied lemon zest
zeste d'orange, orange zest
zewelwai, onion & cream tart from Alsace

vin gris means grey wine...

Vin.

Waterzooi is a Belgian specialty.

charlotte à la framboise

Restaurants

Listed below are restaurants known for serving regional specialties. Phone numbers, days closed and hours of operation often change, so it's advisable to check ahead. Restaurants in tourist areas may have different hours and days of operation during low season.

Reservations are recommended for all restaurants unless noted. The telephone country code for France is 33. When calling outside of your area code in France you must dial a 0 before the area code. You do not use the 0 before the area code when calling France from the USA or Canada. **Prices are for a three-course fixed-priced dinner per person (including tax and service) and without wine.** Lunch, even at the most expensive restaurants listed below, always has a lower fixed price. Credit cards accepted unless noted.

Inexpensive: under $25
Moderate: $26 - $50
Expensive:$51 - $75
Very Expensive: over $75

We think, hope and pray that our restaurant list is current & correct, but remember... things change. Call first or do a "walk by" in the afternoon. Stop in, make a reservation— they'll love you for it.

Aix-en-Provence
Le Bistro Latin
18 rue de la Couronne
04/42382288 (also fax number)
Closed Sun. & Mon. (lunch)
Provençal cuisine at this popular bistro.
Inexpensive-moderate

carpe.

102

Les Bacchanales
10 rue de la Couronne
04/42272106 (also fax number)
Closed Wed. & Thurs. (lunch)
In the old town, this small
restaurant is great for lunch.
Moderate

Angers
Touissant
7 place Kennedy
02/41874620
fax 02/41879664
Closed Sun. (dinner), Mon.,
Feb. vacation & Sept. 1 to 15.
View the château from this
Loire Valley favorite.
Moderate

Ail.

Antibes
Le Brûlot
3 rue Frédéric-Isnard
04/93341776
Closed Sun., Mon. (lunch), late
Aug. & Christmas holiday.
Crowded, hectic bistro near the
market, serving authentic fare.
Moderate

La Taverne du Safranier
place Safranier
Closed Mon. No credit cards.
04/93348050

Informal and inexpensive bistro
serving provençal specialties.
Inexpensive

Arles
Le Vaccarès
9-11 rue Favorin (place du
Forum)
04/90960617
fax 04/90962452
Closed Sun. (dinner), Mon.,
part of Jan. & part of Feb.
Reasonably priced provençal
dishes at this attractive restaurant. Reservations a must.
Moderate

Arnay-le-Duc
Chez Camille
1 place Edouard-Herriot
03/80900138
fax 03/80900464
Located in the hotel of the same
name in this small Burgundy
town, this glass-roofed treasure
is worth the trip. The large staff
serves specialties made with
ingredients from the owner's
farm.
Moderate-expensive

Avignon
Brunel
46 rue de la Balance
04/90852483
fax 04/90862667
Closed Sun. & Mon.
A great spot for lunch after visiting the Papal Palace. You might also want to try the Café Mesclun next door for more casual dining.
Moderate-expensive

La Cuisine de Reine
83 rue Joseph-Vernet
04/90859904
fax 04/90857803
Closed Sun. & Mon. (dinner)
Interesting fare at this bistro serving reasonably priced provençal meals.
Moderate

Bayonne
Euskalduna
61 rue Pannecau
05/59592802
Closed Sun., Mon. part of June & part of Oct.
Basque specialties in France's most Basque city.
Moderate

Beaulieu-sur-Mer
Les Agaves
4 avenue Foch
04/93011312 (also fax)
Closed late Nov., Sun. (dinner) & Mon. (except in high season)
Attractive bistro serving regional specialties, especially grilled dishes; known for their pastries.
Moderate

Beaune
Le Gourmandin
8 place Carnot
03/80240788
fax 03/80222742

Cerises.

Closed first two weeks of Aug., mid-Jan. to mid-Feb., Mon. (dinner) in the summer & Wed. (lunch) in the winter.
Nothing fancy at this centrally located restaurant. Try the excellent *boeuf bourguignon*.
Inexpensive-moderate

Les Tontons
22 rue Faubourg Madeleine
03/80241964
Closed Sun. & Mon. (lunch)
Small restaurant off the place Madeleine serving Burgundy specialties.
Moderate

Biarritz
Café de Paris
5 place Bellevue
05/59241953
fax 05/59241820
Closed Nov. to mid-Mar.
The bistro serves French and
Basque cuisine. If you want
more formal dining, there is
also a more expensive restaurant connected to the café.
Moderate

Bonnieux
Le Fournil
5 place Carnot
04/90758362
fax 04/90759619
Closed mid-Nov. to mid- Dec.,
mid-Jan. to mid-Feb. & Mon.
Provençal cuisine located in a
natural grotto.
Moderate

Auberge de l'Aiguebrun
6 kilometers southeast of
Bonnieux (route D36 and
D943)
04/90044700
fax 04/90044701
Closed Tues. & Wed. (lunch)
Provençal specialties at this
farmhouse located in a small
valley near Bonnieux.
Moderate

Bordeaux
Le Vieux Bordeaux
27 rue Buhan
05/56529436
Closed Sat. (lunch), Sun., Aug.
& early Feb.
Nouvelle cuisine and Bordeaux
regional specialties at this popular restaurant in the old town.
Moderate

Bourg-en-Bresse
Au Chalet de Brou
168 boulevard de Brou
04/74222628
fax 04/74247242
Closed Sun.
Across from the Brou church,
this small restaurant serves
Rhône Valley favorites includ-
ing the famous *volaille de
Bresse*.
Moderate

citron.

Bourges
St-Ambroix
Hôtel de Bourbon
boulevard de la République
02/48708000
fax 02/48702122
In the remains of an abbey, this
hotel restaurant is known for its
regional specialties.
Moderate

Caen
Bourride
15 rue du Vaugueux
02/31935076
fax 02/31932963
Closed Mon., Sun. (dinner),
part of Jan. & Aug.
Highly praised, somewhat formal restaurant (jacket and tie)
serving the best of Normandy.
The restaurant takes its name
from a fish stew.
Expensive-very expensive

Cancale
La Cancalaise
quai Gambetta
02/99896193
fax 2/99898924
Closed Sun. (dinner) & Mon.
Inexpensive restaurant serving
specialties of Brittany. Stop in

after a trip to the Museum of
Oysters!
Moderate

Maison de Bricourt
1 rue Duguesclin
02/99896476
fax 2/99898847
Closed mid-Dec. to mid-Mar.,
Tues. & Wed. (lunch)
Regional specialties in this picturesque fishing port.
Expensive-very expensive

Cannes
Aux Bons Enfants
80 rue Meynadier
No telephone. No credit cards.
Closed Sun., Aug. & Sat. (din-
ner) off-season
Small café near the port serving
simple home-cooked meals.
Inexpensive

La Mère Besson
13 rue des Frères-Pradignac
04/93395924
fax 04/92180358
Closed Sat. (lunch), Mon.
(lunch) & Sun.
Old favorite with outdoor seat-
ing serving provençal dishes.
Moderate

Carcassone

Auberge de Dame Carcas
3 place Château
04/68712323
fax 04/68797967
Closed mid-Jan. to mid-Feb.,
Mon. & Tues. (lunch)
You can eat well and inexpen-
sively on the terrace of this
popular restaurant serving specialties of Roussillon.
Inexpensive

Le Languedoc
32 allée d'Iéna
04/68252217
fax 04/68471322
Closed summer Sun. (dinner),
Mon. & mid-Dec. to mid-Jan.
Indoor and outdoor dining at
this attractive restaurant.
Moderate

Carpentras

Auberge du Beaucet
7 miles southeast of Carpentras.
Route D4 to D39 in Beaucet.
04/90661082
fax 04/90660072
Closed Sun. (dinner), Mon.,
Dec. & Jan.
Straightforward provençal
cuisine stressing fresh local

ingredients. It's a little out of
the way but worth it.
Moderate

Cassis

Jardin d'Emile
plage du Bestouan
04/42018055
fax 04/42018070
Closed Sun. (dinner) from Nov.
to Feb.
Regional specialties served on
the terrace of this small hotel.
Moderate

Chamonix

Maison Carrier
route du Bouchet
04/50530003
fax 04/50559548
Closed mid- Nov. to mid-Dec.,
Mon. (except July & Aug.)
This restaurant draws from the
cuisine of France, Italy and
Switzerland.
Moderate

Chantilly

La Ferme de Condé
42 av. du Maréchal-Joffre
03/44573231
Closed Tues.
Try lunch in this elegant restau-

rant - once a chapel - while visiting the Renaissance château.
Moderate

Chartres
Le Buisson Ardent
10 rue au Lait
02/37340466
fax 02/37911582
Closed Sun. (dinner)
Specialties of the Ile-de-France region served in an old and attractive restaurant near the gothic Cathédrale Notre-Dame
Moderate

Châteauneuf-du-Pape
Le Pistou
15 rue Joseph-Ducos
04/90837175
fax 04/90149504
Closed Sun. (dinner) & Mon.
Provençal cuisine indoors and outdoors. The restaurant takes its name from pistou (pesto).
Inexpensive-moderate

Cogolin (near Saint-Tropez)
La Ferme du Magnan
route 98
04/94495754
Closed Tues.
Ten minutes from Saint Tropez,

this restaurant specializes in provençal food and is located on a farm. Definitely worth the drive. Open April to November.
Moderate

Colmar
Caveau Hansi
23 rue des Marchands
03/89413784 (also fax number)
Closed Wed., Thurs. & Jan.
This traditional tavern in the old town serves Alsatian specialties.
Moderate

Crepon
Ferme de la Rançonnière
Route d'Arromanches
02/31222173
fax 02/31229839
Dine fire-side on lobster (*homard*) and the specialties of Normandy at this hotel/restaurant located in a comfortable, old manor house.
Moderate

← We had a great meal here & a wonderful time, despite the approximately 75 children running loose.

Dijon

La Toison d'Or
18 rue Ste-Anne
03/80307352
fax 03/80309551
Closed Sun. (dinner)
An elegant restaurant serving regional specialties.
Moderate

Le Pré aux Clercs
13 place de la Libération
03/80380505
fax 03/80381616
Closed Sun. (dinner), Mon. & part of Aug.
The specialties of Burgundy are served in this restaurant located across from the Palais de Ducs. Large selection of wines from Burgundy.
Expensive

Dinan

Mère Pourcel
3 place des Merciers
02/96390380
fax 02/96394991
Closed Feb., Sun. (dinner) & Mon. (part of the year)
Specialties of Brittany at this 15th-century restaurant.
Moderate-expensive

Dinard

Présidence
29 boulevard du Président-Wilson
02/99464427 (also fax number)
Closed around Christmas, Feb., Sun. (dinner) & Mon.
Attractive restaurant specializing in seafood in this Brittany resort town.
Inexpensive-moderate

Daurade.

Eze

Le Troubadour
4 rue du Brec
04/93411903
Closed part of July, Aug. & late Nov. to mid- Dec.
Unpretentious restaurant serving regional fare in this tourist town.
Moderate

Hostellerie du Château de la
Chèvre d'Or
rue du Barri
04/92106666
fax 04/93410672
Closed mid-Nov. to Feb.
This incredible hotel complex
of stone houses has three
restaurants: Restaurant de la
Chèvre d'Or (very expensive),
Olivetta (moderate Italian trat-
toria) and Le Grill (moderate).
If you don't eat here, have a
drink and watch the sunset.

Fayence

Patin Couffin
Placette Olivier
04/94762996
Regional cuisine in this attrac-
tive Provence hilltop village.
Inexpesnive-moderate

Figeac

Cuisine du Marché
15 rue Clermont
05/65501855 (also fax number)
Closed Sun.
The cuisine of the Périgord
region (especially *canard*)
served in this village in
Southwestern France.
Inexpensive-moderate

Fontainebleau

La Route du Beaujolais
3 rue Montebello
01/64222798
Inexpensive dining near the
famous château.
Inexpensive-moderate

Gémenos

Le Relais de la Magdelaine
Route d'Aix-en-Provence
(N396)
04/42322016
fax 04/42320226
Closed mid-Nov. to mid-Mar.
Provençal cuisine served in this
18th-century country hotel.
Moderate

Giverny

Jardins de Giverny
1 rue Milieu
02/32216080
fax 02/32519377
Closed Feb. & Mon. Dinners
Sat. only
On a day trip to Monet's house,
try lunch outside.
Moderate

figue.

Grenoble

Brasserie de Strasbourg
11 avenue Alsace-Lorraine
04/76461803 (also fax number)
Closed Sun., Mon. (dinner) &
part of Aug.
Reasonably priced, consistently
good meals on your way to see
the French Alps.
Inexpensive

Grimaud

Le Côteau Fleuri
place des Pénitents
04/944332017
fax 04/94433342
Closed mid-Nov. to mid-Dec.,
first part of Jan. & Tues.
(except in July & Aug.)
Attractive hotel/restaurant
located on the quiet place des
Pénitents.
Moderate

La Bretonnière
place des Pénitents
04/94432526
Closed in off-season on some
evenings.
Traditional fare at this lovely
restaurant in quiet Grimaud.
Moderate

Honfleur

L'Assiette Gourmande
2 quai des Passagers
02/31892488
fax 02/31899017
A favorite of travelers to
Normandy and lovers of
seafood, especially scallops.
Moderate-expensive

L'Isle-sur-la-Sourge

Lou Nego Chin
12 quai Jean-Jaurès
04/90208803
Closed Sun. (dinner) & Mon.
We loved this restaurant and
dined in both the tiny restaurant
and outdoor on a deck over the
river.
Inexpensive-moderate

Caveau de la Tour de L'Isle
12 rue de la République
04/90207025
Wine store and bar. You can try
wines by the glass (accompanied by complimentary cheese
and sausage).
Inexpensive

Lyon

Hugon
12 rue Pizay
04/78281094
Closed weekends & Aug.
This small *bouchon* (tavern)
serves inexpensive regional
cuisine.
Inexpensive

Paul Bocuse
50 quai de la Plage (in
Collognes-au-Mont-d'Or)
04/72429090
fax 04/72278587
Reservations far in advance.
Jacket & tie.
Lyon is known in France and
around the world for its rich
cuisine and this, to many, is the
best in the Lyonnaise tradition.
Very expensive

Le Nord
18 rue Nueve
04/72106969
fax 04/72106968
Historic downtown brasserie
serving authentic fare of Lyon.
Inexpensive-moderate

Marseillan

Chez Philippe
20 rue Suffren
04/67017062 (also fax)
Closed Sun. (dinner) & Mon. &
Tues. in off-season
Wonderful food in an intimate
setting in this fishing village.
Inexpensive

Marseille

Les Arcenaulx
25 cours Estienne d'Orves
04/91598030
fax 04/91547633
Closed Sun.
Provençal cuisine near the port
with outdoor dining. You can
visit the connected bookstore.
Moderate

Mont-St-Michel

Le Mère Poularde
Grande Rue
02/33601401
Cuisine of Normandy, especially *agneau pré salé* (from lambs
which graze at the base of the
abbey).
Moderate-expensive

les olives.

Mouthier-Haute-Pierre
La Cascade
route des Gorges de Noailles
03/81609530
fax 03/81609455
Closed mid-Nov. to mid-Feb.
Regional specialties (especially
trout) of the Jura mountain area
served in this unspoiled village
on a gorge overlooking the
Loue River (southeast of
Besançon). The restaurant has
little charm, but at least it is no
smoking (a rarity in France).
Moderate

Nancy
Au P'tit Cuny
97 Grande Rue
03/83328594
Closed Sun. & Mon.
Experience the cuisine of
Lorraine (especially sauerkraut-
based dishes).
Inexpensive

Nantes
La Cigale
4 place Graslin
02/51849494
fax 02/51849495
This brasserie is a historic land-
mark located across from the

Théâtre Graslin and features the
specialties of Brittany.
Inexpensive

Nevers
Cour St-Étienne
33 rue St-Étienne
03/86367457
Closed Sun. (dinner), Mon.
(lunch), Aug. & part of Jan.
Indoor and outdoor dining at
this restaurant known for serving the specialties of Burgundy.
Inexpensive-moderate

Nice
La Cambuse
5 Cours Saleya
04/93801231
Closed Sun. & Mon.
Located on the busy Cours
Saleya, this restaurant serves
traditional niçoise dishes.
Moderate

Le Chantecler
37 Promenade des Anglais
04/93166400
fax 04/93883568
Elegant dining in the famous
Hôtel Négresco.
Very Expensive

Choupette *great place!*
20 rue Barillerie
04/93802869
Traditional niçoise food at this
restaurant located on the street
behind the Cours Saleya.
Moderate

Le Bistro des Artistes
13 Bis Cours Saleya
04/93856191
Open-air bistro serving niçoise
dishes.
Moderate

Don Camillo
5 rue des Ponchettes
04/93856795
fax 04/93139743
Closed Sun., Mon. (lunch) &
late July to early Aug.
Located off the Cours Saleya in
old Nice and specializing in
local dishes.
Moderate

La Merenda
4 rue de la Terrasse
Closed weekends, parts of Feb.
& Aug. & Christmas holiday.
No credit cards.
Niçoise dishes served at this
authentic Nice bistro.

Reservations essential. No
phone. Always crowded.
Moderate

La Pérouse
11 quai Rauba-Capéu
04/93623463
fax 4/93625941
Closed winter.
Dine on niçoise specialties in
the garden of this popular hotel
at the foot of the château-fort.
Moderate-Expensive

Le Safari
1 Cours Saleya
04/93801844
Closed Mon. (in winter)
Provençal and niçoise specialties at this popular restaurant
overlooking the flower market.
We ate here frequently and
never had a bad meal. The people-watching is great.
Inexpensive-Moderate

Ornans

Hôtel de France
51-53 rue Pierre-Vernier
03/81622444
fax 03/81621203
Exquisite meal in an out-of-the-
way place in this hotel/restau-

rant located in an unspoiled town in the Franche-Comté region. Trout and game dishes are featured on the menu.
Moderate

Paris

Allard
6th/Métro St-Michel
41 rue St-André-des-Arts
01/43264823
fax 01/46330402
Closed Sun. & part of Aug.
Diners repeatedly praise the service and food at this bistro.
Moderate

Baracane
4th/Métro Bastille
38 rue des Tournelles
01/42714333
Closed Sat. (lunch) & Sun.
Small restaurant in the Marais featuring the specialties of Southwest France (especially *confit*).
Inexpensive-moderate

Bistro 121
15th/Métro Boucicaut
121 rue Convention
01/45575290
fax 01/45571469

Closed some Mon.
A favorite of many visitors seeking a romantic, elegant evening in a French bistro.
Moderate

Bistro de Deux Théâtres
9th/Métro Blanche
18 rue Blanche
01/45264143
fax 01/48740892
Affordable dining with locals at this neighborhood bistro.
Moderate

Bofinger
4th/Métro Bastille
5 rue de la Bastille
01/42728782
fax 01/42729768
Open until 1 a.m.
Glass-roofed brasserie located between the place des Vosges and the place de la Bastille.
Inexpensive-moderate

persil.

Bonne Fourchette
1st/Métro Tuileries
320 rue St-Honoré
01/42604527
Closed Sat., Sun., Aug. & part of Feb.
Typical Parisian restaurant serving traditional cuisine at reasonable prices.
Moderate

Les Bouchons de François Clerc ☆☆
12 rue Hôtel Colbert
5th/ Métro Maubert-Mutualité
01/43541534
fax 01/46346807
Closed lunch & Sun.
Our French editor Marie Fossier recommended this restaurant and everyone we have sent there has loved it (especially the cheese course).
Moderate

Brasserie Flo
10th/Métro Château d'Eau
7 cour des Petites-Écuries
01/47701359
fax 01/42470080
Open daily until 1.30 a.m. Alsatian food and Parisian atmosphere at this 1886

brasserie. On a passageway near Gare de l'Est.
Moderate

Campagne et Provence
5th/Métro Maubert-Mutualité
25 quai de la Tournelle
01/43540517
Closed Mon. (lunch), Sat. (lunch) & Sun.
Small restaurant on the quai across from Notre Dame providing provençal cuisine to the visitor to Paris.
Moderate

A la votre!

Chardenoux
11th/Métro Charonne
1 rue Jules-Valles
01/43714952
Closed weekends & Aug.
Traditional Parisian cooking in the Bastille/République. Game dishes are popular here.
Moderate

Chartier
9th/Métro rue Montmartre
7 rue du Faubourg-Montmartre
01/47708629
No credit cards.
Traditional Paris soup kitchen with affordable prices. The

tripes à la mode de Caen is a frequent special of the day (we passed on that). Lots of tourists and you may be seated with strangers which we really enjoy and is a great way to meet people.
Inexpensive

Chez Paul
11th/Métro Bastille
13 rue de Charonne
01/47003457
Our favorite bistro in Paris. No tourists, never a bad meal (try the rabbit) and ask to eat upstairs.
Moderate

L'Été en Pente Douce
18th/Métro Château-Rouge
23 rue Muller
Near Sacré-Coeur, this interesting and picturesque café is where we met one of our favorite Parisiennes - Loralyn.
Inexpensive

Fauchon
8th/Métro Madeleine
26 place de la Madeleine
01/47426011
Deli and grocery known for its

huge collection of canned food, bakery and alcohol. The store is a must for those wanting to bring back French specialties. There are also five restaurants on the premises ranging in price from inexpensive to expensive.

La Flèche d'Or Café
20th/Métro Alexandre-Dumas/Porte de Bagnolet
102B rue de Bagnolet
01/43720423
Funky café/nightclub located in a former train station. Limited menu.
Inexpensive

Au Gamin de Paris
4th/Métro Saint-Paul
49/51 rue Vielle du Temple
01/42789724
Small Marais restaurant serving Parisian specialties.
Moderate

Jo Goldenberg
4th/Métro Saint-Paul
7 rue des Rosiers
01/48872016
Take-out and restaurant at this Jewish deli in the Marais that

became more famous for the wrong reason (the bombing by anti-Semitic terrorists in the early 1980s).
Inexpensive

Juvenile's
1st/Métro Bourse
47 rue de Richelieu
01/42974649
Closed Sun.
Around the corner from Willi's Wine Bar, this inexpensive, unpretentious restaurant serves light meals and has a large wine selection.
Inexpensive

Ma Bourgogne *great place!*
1st/Métro Saint-Paul
19 place des Vosges
01/42784464
This café/restaurant in the Place des Vosges (the oldest square in Paris) serves traditional Parisian cuisine and specializes in roast chicken.
Moderate

Au Monde de Chimères
4th/Métro Cite or Ponte Marie
69 rue St-Louis-en L'Ile
01/43544527

fax 01/43298488
Closed Sun. & Mon.
Small restaurant with great food and pleasant service.
Moderate

Pause Café
11th/Métro Ledru-Rollin
41 rue de Charonne
01/48068033
Popular café specializing in *tourtes*.
Inexpensive

Perraudin
5th/Métro Luxembourg or Cluny-La Sorbonne
157 rue Saint-Jacques
No reservations. No credit cards.
01/46331575
You'll get to know your fellow diners at this inexpensive bistro serving traditional Parisian cuisine.
Inexpensive

Au Petit Riche
9th/Métro Le Peletier
25 rue Le Peletier
01/47706868
fax 01/48241079
Closed Sun.

mache.

118

This bistro serves specialties of the Loire Valley with a Parisian twist.
Moderate

Polidor
6th/Métro Odéon
41 rue Monsieur-le-Prince
01/43269534
No reservations. No credit cards.
Popular 1930's bistro serving inexpensive traditional Parisian cuisine.
Inexpensive

Procope
6th/Métro Odéon
13 rue de l'Ancienne Comédie
01/40467900
fax 01/40467909
Open everyday to 1 a.m.
Oldest brasserie in Paris located in the Saint-Germain des Près area. Parisian cuisine at affordable prices served in small dining rooms.
Inexpensive-moderate

La Ravaldière
7th/Métro Rue de Bac
1 rue Saint-Simon
01/45485396

French country cooking near the Boulevard Saint-Germain. Don't come here if you don't like dogs as there is always a dog in the restaurant. The 100-francs menu at lunch and dinner is a great deal.
Inexpensive

Le Soufflé
1st/Métro Tuileries
36 rue du Mont-Thabor
(between places Vendôme and Concorde)
01/42602719
fax 01/42605498
Closed Sun.
The name is deceiving as this restaurant, known for its *soufflé*, has a full menu.
Moderate

Le Train Bleu
12th/Métro Gare-de-Lyon
In the Gare de Lyon train station.
20 boulevard Diderot
01/43430906
fax 01/43439796
Forget all the food you have eaten in train stations. But you don't really come here for the food because the setting, with

These restaurants are very expensive and highly praised. You will find them in nearly every other guide book. Reservations well in advance are a must as are jacket and tie:

Alain Ducasse
16th/Métro Trocadéro
59 avenue Raymond-Poincaré
01/47271227
fax 01/47273122
Closed mid-July to mid-Aug., Dec.24-Jan 4 & weekends.

L'Ambroisie
4th/Métro St-Paul
9 place des Vosges
01/42785145
Closed first three weeks of Aug, part of Feb. & Sun. & Mon.

L'Arpège
7th/Métro Varenne
84 rue de Varenne
01/45514733
fax 01/44189839
Closed weekends.

Guy Savoy
17th/Métro Charles-de-Gaulle-Étoile
18 rue Troyon
01/43804061
fax 01/46224309
Closed Sat. (lunch) & Sun.

Lucas-Carton
8th/Métro Madeleine
9 place Madeleine
01/42652290
fax 01/42650623
Closed first three weeks of Aug, Mon. & Sat.for lunch & Sun.

Pierre Gagnaire
8th/Métro Charles-de-Gaulle-Étoile
6 rue Balzac (Hôtel Balzac)
01/44351825
fax 01/44351837
Closed mid-July to mid-Aug., Christmas vacation, Feb. vacation, Sun (lunch) & Sat.

Taillevent
8th/Métro Charles-de-Gaulle-Étoile
15 rue Lamennais
01/44951501
fax 01/42259518
Closed July 24-Aug. 24, weekends & holidays

Tour d'Argent
5th/Métro Maubert
15 quai de al Tournelle (with a view of Notre-Dame)
01/43542331
fax 01/44071204
Closed Mon.

its murals of the French-speaking world, is spectacular.
Moderate

La Truffe
4th/Métro Saint-Paul
31 rue Vieille-du-Temple
01/42710839
Looking for vegetarian, low-fat Parisian cuisine? This is the place. There is no smoking at this restaurant (a rarity in Paris).
Inexpensive

Willi's Wine Bar
1st/Métro Bourse
13 rue des Petits-Champs
01/42610509
fax 01/47033693
Closed Sun.
British owners serve Parisian specialties. A great wine list and a favorite of one of our "research assistants."
Moderate

Pérouges
Ostellerie du Vieux Pérouges
place Tilleul
04/74610088
fax 04/74347790
Local specialties of medieval Pérouges served in a 13th-century inn.
Moderate-expensive

Perpignan
Casa Sansa
4 rue Fabrique Couverte
04/68342184
fax 04/68351965
Closed Sun.
Catalan food (including paella) at this interesting bistro. A little bit of Spain while you visit France.
Inexpensive

un aperatif.

Poitiers
Maxime
4 rue St-Nicolas
05/49410955 (also fax number)
Closed weekends & mid-July to mid-Aug.
Specialties of the Poitou-Charentes region at this attractive restaurant.
Moderate-expensive

Reims
Boyer
64 boulevard Vasnier
03/26828080
03/26826552
Closed Mon. & Tues. (lunch)

Formal, luxurious, very expensive and highly praised restaurant known for its extensive wine list. Reservations well in advance are a must.
Very expensive

Le Vigneron
place Paul-Jamot
03/26798686
fax 03/26798687
Closed Sat. (lunch), Sun., first part of Aug. & Christmas holiday.
The regional specialties of Champagne are served at this reasonably priced restaurant.
Inexpensive-Moderate

Rennes
Piccadilly Tavern
15 Galeries du Théâtre
02/99781717
This inexpensive tavern is a favorite of tourists and features fresh seafood.
Inexpensive

Four à Ban
4 rue St-Mélaine
02/99387285 (also fax number)
Closed part of Feb., part of Aug, weekends

A favorite of locals and known for good food at reasonable prices.
Moderate

Ribeauville
Caveau de l'Ami Fritz
1 place Ancien Hôpital
03/89736811
Inexpensive and casual restaurant serving Alsatian specialties, especially game.
Inexpensive

Rocamadour
Le Beau Site
Cité Médiévale
05/65336308
fax 05/65336523
Closed some Sun. and in off-season.
Overlooking the canyon, this hotel restaurant in the old town stays away from the tourist fare of most restaurants in this popular tourist destination.
Moderate

Roquebrune-Cap-Martin
Le Roquebrune
100 avenue J. Jaurés (Basse-Corniche)
04/93350016

morille

fax 04/93289836
Closed Nov., mid-June and
Aug. (except Sat. & Sun.)
One of the highest-praised
restaurants on the Côte d'Azur.
The terrace overlooks the coast
and the view and the food are
excellent.
Expensive-very expensive

Rouen

La Toque d'Or
11 place du Vieux-Marché
02/35714629
Large bistro (next to the mod-
ern Joan of Arc church) with a
large menu of Normandy specialties.
Moderate

St-Émilion

Francis Goullée
rue Guadet
05/57247049
fax 05/57744796
Closed Sun. (dinner) & Mon.
Comfortable restaurant serving
Bordeaux regional favorites,
especially dishes featuring
duck.
Moderate

Chez Germaine
13 rue du Clocher
05/57744934
Closed Sun. & Mon.
Indoor and outdoor dining on
regional favorites of Bordeaux.
Moderate

Logis de la Cadène
Place du Marché
05/57247140
fax 05/57744223
Closed Sun. (dinner) & Mon.
Regional specialties in this
charming wine village.
Moderate

St-Jean Cap-Ferrat

Le Provençal
2 avenue Denis-Séméria
04/93760397
Closed mid-Oct. to Feb.
Overlooking the port of this
beautiful town, serving
provençal dishes.
Moderate-expensive

Le Sloop
Au Nouveau Port
04/93014863
Closed Wed. (dinner) in off-
season & mid-Nov. to mid-Dec.
Reasonably priced dining on

the port.
Inexpensive-moderate

St-Malo ✗

Duchesse Anne
Place Guy la Chambre
02/99408533
fax 02/99400028
Closed Wed. & Dec. & Jan.
Located within the walls of the
old town, this beautiful and historic restaurant specializes in
lobster and steaks. We had the
kidneys (thinking we had
ordered steak).
Moderate

St Rémy-de-Provence

Xa
24 boulevard Mirabeau
04/90924123
Closed Wed.
Popular restaurant frequented
by locals and specializing in
provençal dishes.
Inexpensive-moderate

St Tropez

L'Echalote
35 rue Allard
04/94548326
Closed mid-Nov. to mid-Dec.
Well-known restaurant serving

the dishes of South and
Southwestern France, especial-
ly meat dishes.
Inexpensive-moderate

La Bouillabaisse
plage de la Bouillabaisse
04/94975400
Indoor and beachfront dining at
this restaurant specializing in
grilled seafood and including,
of course, *bouillabaisse*.
Moderate-expensive

Sarlat

Rapière
place Cathédrale
05/53590313
fax 05/53302784
Closed Sun., part of Jan. & part
of Feb.
Outdoor dining near the cathedral in this picturesque
Dordogne town.
Moderate

Chocolat chaud.

Strasburg

Brasserie de l'Ancienne
Douane
6 rue de la Douane
03/88157878
fax 03/88224564
Closed most of Jan.

Large brasserie in the old town serving Alsatian specialties. Inexpensive-moderate

Le Buerehiesel
4 parc de l'Orangerie
03/88455665
fax 03/88613200
Closed Tues. & Wed., Aug. & some holiday weeks.
Reservations a must.
This (somewhat stuffy) restaurant located in a farm house is known for Alsatian cuisine, especially *foie gras*.
Very Expensive

Le Clou
3 rue Chaudron
03/88321167
fax 03/88757283
Closed Wed. (lunch), Sun. & holidays
This wine bar (*Winstub*) serves traditional Alsatian dishes such as *waedele* (pork knuckle).
Moderate

Fink' Stuebel
26 rue Finkwiller
03/88250757
fax 03/88221105
Closed Sun. (dinner), Mon.,

part of Jan., Feb. & Aug.
A wine bar (*Winstub*) serving Alsatian specialties such as onion tart (*tarte à l'oignon)* and noodle dumplings (*spätzle*) at reasonable prices.
Inexpensive-moderate

Toulouse
Chez Emile
13 pl. St-Georges
05/61210556
fax 05/61214226
Closed Sun., Mon. & end of Aug.
Featuring Toulouse specialties such as *cassoulet*.
Moderate

Tours
Les Tuffeaux
19 rue Lavoisier
02/47471989
Closed Sun. & Mon. (lunch)
The specialities of the Loire Valley and the château country are served in this restaurant.
Moderate

Trouville
Les Vapeurs
160 boulevard Moureaux
02/31881524

Art-deco brasserie facing the port with indoor and outdoor dining on Normandy specialties. Inexpensive-moderate

Val-de-Mercy
Auberge du Château
3 rue du Pont
03/86416000
fax 03/86417328
Closed Sun. (dinner) & Mon. Located in a renovated inn in this quiet village, this small, elegant restaurant serves the specialties of Burgundy. Moderate-expensive

Vezelay
L'Auberge de la Coquille
81 rue Saint-Pierre
03/86333557
fax 03/86333784
Located near the basilica, this is a good spot for lunch in this Burgundian tourist town. Regional specialties are served in the restaurant and terrace. Inexpensive-moderate

Vence
La Farigoule
15 rue Henri-Isnard
04/93580127
Closed Wed. (lunch)
Classic provençal cuisine with indoor and outdoor dining. Moderate

Vienne
Le Bec Fin
7 place St-Maurice
04/74857672
fax 04/74851530
Closed Sun. (dinner), Mon., part of Aug. & Christmas holiday.
A good value near the cathedral. Jacket and reservations a must. Moderate

Villefranche-sur-Mer
La Mère Germaine
quai Courbet
04/93017139
fax 04/93769428
Closed mid-Nov. to late Dec. Café/restaurant on the waterfront specializing in grilled fish dishes. Moderate

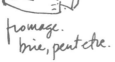

fromage.
brie, peut être.

Invitation for Comments:

We like to think that we have been as thorough as possible, but we welcome any and all comments, additions and corrections from our readers. And we'd love to hear about any restaurants you find off the beaten path. You can reach us at:

> What Kind of Food Am I?
> 8223 N. Gray Log Lane
> Milwaukee, WI 53217-2863
> USA
> Fax: 1-414-228-4917
> e-mail: EATnDRINK@aol.com
> www.eatndrink.com

About the Authors:
Michael Dillon, when not operating his graphic-design firm, is planning his next meal. Design and illustrations in this guide are the work of Mr. Dillon.

Andy Herbach, when not engaged in the practice of law, is planning his next trip.

Both authors reside in Milwaukee, Wisconsin.

NOTES

Winston.